Careers in Focus

Careers in Focus

ADVERTISING
AND
MARKETING

SECOND EDITION

Ferguson

An imprint of Infobase Publishing

Ferguson
An imprint of Infobase Publishing
132 West 31st Street
New York NY 10001

Library of Congress Cataloging-in-Publication Data

Careers in focus. Advertising and marketing. — 2nd ed.
    p. cm. — (Careers in focus)
  Rev. ed. of: Careers in focus. Advertising & marketing. 2004.
  Includes bibliographical references and index.
  ISBN-13: 978-0-8160-7295-8 (alk. paper)
  ISBN-10: 0-8160-7295-7 (alk. paper)
  1. Advertising—Vocational guidance—Juvenile literature. 2. Marketing—Vocational guidance—Juvenile literature. I. Careers in focus. Advertsing & marketing. II. Title: Advertising and marketing.
  HF5828.4.C374 2008
  658.80023'73—dc22
                    2008031650

Ferguson books are available at special discounts when purchased in bulk quantities for businesses, associations, institutions, or sales promotions. Please call our Special Sales Department in New York at (212) 967-8800 or (800) 322-8755.

You can find Ferguson on the World Wide Web at http://www.fergpubco.com

Text design by David Strelecky
Cover design by Salvatore Luongo

Printed in the United States of America

Sheridan MSRF 10 9 8 7 6 5 4 3 2 1

This book is printed on acid-free paper.

Table of Contents

Introduction

Advertising is mass communication that a business or organization (the advertiser) purchases to persuade a particular segment of the public to adopt ideas or buy goods or services. Today, advertising agencies prepare most national and local advertising.

Marketing is the practice of anticipating customer needs and directing the flow of need-satisfying goods and services from producer to customer. The business discipline of marketing took shape as sellers realized that product design could be altered to suit the needs of a product's potential buyers, or target market. Sellers also discovered the importance of identifying a group of buyers before starting an advertising campaign. This would enable the producer to tailor the campaign to reach that specific group, which would ultimately increase the chances of launching a successful product. Marketing, therefore, provides a service for both sides of the business world: the seller and the buyer.

Market-driven thinking is now a major part of business decisions and begins long before the product-development, manufacturing, and sales processes. In fact, the market is the central focus of both today's advertising and marketing trends and those that will take industries into the next millennium.

Advertising and marketing grow in direct proportion to the national economy. When the economy is favorable, both industries enjoy considerable growth. Growth can be accelerated through the development of new products and services and the resulting increase in competition among producers of both industrial and consumer goods.

An important trend that affects employment opportunities in the advertising and marketing industries is specialization. Many agencies are focusing on increasingly specific, or niche, markets; this trend will become even more pronounced in the coming years. Expected high-growth areas include campaigns aimed at specific ethnic or age groups, special-events promotions, and direct-marketing campaigns for retailers and technological companies. Advertising and marketing firms are also offering more diverse services (such as public relations, sales, and interactive media services) to attract and retain clients.

Each article in this book discusses in detail a particular advertising or marketing occupation. The articles in *Careers in Focus: Advertising and Marketing* appear in Ferguson's *Encyclopedia of Careers and Vocational Guidance*, but have been updated and revised with the latest information from the U.S. Department of Labor, professional organizations, and other sources.

The following paragraphs detail the sections and features that appear in this book.

The **Quick Facts** section provides a brief summary of the career, including recommended school subjects, personal skills, work environment, minimum educational requirements, salary ranges, certification or licensing requirements, and employment outlook. This section also provides acronyms and identification numbers for the following government classification indexes: the *Dictionary of Occupational Titles* (DOT), the Guide for Occupational Exploration (GOE), the National Occupational Classification (NOC) Index, and the Occupational Information Network (O*NET)-Standard Occupational Classification System (SOC) index. The DOT, GOE, and O*NET-SOC indexes have been created by the U.S. government; the NOC index is Canada's career classification system. Readers can use the identification numbers listed in the Quick Facts section to access further information about a career. Print editions of the DOT (*Dictionary of Occupational Titles.* Indianapolis, Ind.: JIST Works, 1991) and GOE (*Guide for Occupational Exploration.* Indianapolis, Ind.: JIST Works, 2001) are available at libraries. Electronic versions of the NOC (http://www23.hrdc-drhc.gc.ca) and O*NET-SOC (http://online.onetcenter.org) are available on the Internet. When no DOT, GOE, NOC, or O*NET-SOC numbers are present, this means that the U.S. Department of Labor or Human Resources Development Canada have not created a numerical designation for this career. In this instance, you will see the acronym "N/A," or not available.

The **Overview** section is a brief introductory description of the duties and responsibilities involved in this career. Oftentimes, a career may have a variety of job titles. When this is the case, alternative career titles are presented. Employment statistics are also provided, when available. The **History** section describes the history of the particular job as it relates to the overall development of its industry or field. **The Job** describes the primary and secondary duties of the job. **Requirements** discusses high school and postsecondary education and training requirements, any certification or licensing that is necessary, and other personal requirements for success in the job. **Exploring** offers suggestions on how to gain experience in or knowledge of the particular job before making a firm educational and financial commitment. The focus is on what can be done while still in high school (or in the early years of college) to gain a better understanding of the job. The **Employers** section gives an overview of typical places of employment for the job. **Starting Out** discusses the best ways to land that first job, be it through the college career services office, newspaper ads, Internet employment sites, or personal contact. The **Advancement** section describes what kind of career path to expect from the job and how to get there. **Earnings** lists salary ranges and describes the typical fringe benefits. The **Work Environment** section describes the typical surroundings and conditions of employment—whether indoors or outdoors, noisy or quiet, social or independent. Also discussed are typical hours worked, any seasonal fluctuations, and the stresses and strains of the job. The **Outlook** section summarizes the job in terms of the general economy and industry projections. For the most part, Outlook information is obtained from the U.S. Bureau of Labor Statistics and is supplemented by information gathered from professional associations. Job growth terms follow those used in the *Occupational Outlook Handbook*. Growth described as "much faster than the average" means an increase of 21 percent or more. Growth described as "faster than the average" means an increase of 14 to 20 percent. Growth described as "about as fast as the average" means an increase of 7 to 13 percent. Growth described as "more slowly than the average" means an increase of 3 to 6 percent. "Little or no change" means a decrease of 2 percent to an increase of 2 percent. "Decline" means a decrease of 3 percent or more. Each article ends with **For More Information,** which lists organizations that provide information on training, education, internships, scholarships, and job placement.

Careers in Focus: Advertising and Marketing also includes photographs, informative sidebars, and interviews with professionals in the field.

Advertising Account Executives

OVERVIEW

Advertising account executives coordinate and oversee everything related to a client's advertising account and act as the primary liaison between the agency and the client. They are also responsible for building and maintaining professional relationships among clients and coworkers to ensure the successful completion of major ad campaigns and the assurance of continued business with clients. Advertising account executives and related workers hold 170,000 jobs in the United States.

HISTORY

When the advertising industry formally developed in the late 1800s, advertisers themselves were usually the ones who handled the promotion of their products and services, placing ads in newspapers and magazines to reach their customers. As the number of newspapers increased and print advertising became more widespread, however, these advertisers called on specialists who knew how to create and coordinate effective advertisements. One such specialist, the advertising account executive, emerged to produce and handle the ad campaigns for businesses.

Advertising agencies were commonly used by companies by the 1920s, and account executives worked for such agencies. Together with a staff of creative professionals, the account executive was able to develop an advertising "package," including slogans, jingles, and images, as well as a general campaign strategy. In addition, account executives did basic market research, oversaw the elements that went into a campaign, and worked hand-in-hand with writers and artists to develop effective ads for their clients.

Today, account executives handle all aspects of their clients' ad campaigns. As a result, they bring to the job a broad base of knowledge, including account management, marketing, sales promotion, merchandising, client accounting, print production, public relations, and the creative arts.

THE JOB

Account executives track the day-to-day progress of the overall advertising campaigns of their clients. Together with a staff commonly consisting of a creative director, an art director, a copywriter, researchers, and production specialists, the account executive monitors all client accounts from beginning to end.

Before an advertising campaign is actually launched, a lot of preparatory work is needed. Account executives must familiarize themselves with their clients' products and services, target markets, goals, competitors, and preferred media. Together with the agency team, the account executive conducts research and holds initial meetings with clients. Then the team, coordinated by the account executive, uses this information to analyze market potential and presents recommendations to the client.

After an advertising strategy has been determined and all terms have been agreed upon, the agency's creative staff goes to work, developing ideas and producing various ads to present to the client. During this time, the account executive works with *media buyers* (who purchase radio and television time and publication space for advertising) to develop a schedule for the project and make sure that the costs involved are within the client's budget.

When the ad campaign has been approved by the client, production can begin. In addition to supervising and coordinating the work of copywriters, editors, graphic artists, production specialists, and other employees on the agency team, the account executive must also write reports and draft business correspondence, follow up on all client meetings, interact with outside vendors, and ensure that all pieces of the advertising campaign clearly communicate the desired message. In sum, the account executive is responsible for making sure that the client is satisfied. This may require making modifications to the campaign, revising cost estimates and events schedules, and redirecting the efforts of the creative staff.

In addition to their daily responsibilities of tracking and handling clients' advertising campaigns, account executives must also develop and bring in new business, keep up to date on current advertising trends, evaluate the effectiveness of advertising programs, and track sales figures.

REQUIREMENTS

High School

You can prepare for a career as an advertising account executive by taking a variety of courses at the high school level. Basic courses in business, communication, economics, English, journalism, mathematics, psychology, and social science are important for aspiring advertising account executives.

Postsecondary Training

Most advertising agencies hire college graduates whose degrees can vary widely, from English, journalism, or marketing to business administration, fine arts, or speech communications. Courses in business, economics, psychology, sociology, and any art medium are helpful. Some positions require a graduate degree in advertising, art, or marketing. Others may call for experience in a particular field, such as health care, insurance, or retail.

While most employers prefer a broad liberal arts background with courses in communication, consumer behavior, marketing, market research, sales, and technology, many also seek employees who already have some work experience. Candidates who have completed on-the-job internships at agencies or have developed portfolios will have a competitive edge.

Other Requirements

While account executives do not need to have the same degree of artistic skill or knowledge as art directors or graphic designers, they must be imaginative and understand the communication of art and photography to direct the overall progress of an ad campaign. They should also be able to work under pressure, motivate employees, solve problems, and demonstrate flexibility, good judgment, decisiveness, and patience.

Account executives must be aware of trends and be interested in the business climate and the psychology of making purchases. In addition, they should be able to write clearly, make effective presentations, and communicate persuasively. It is also helpful to stay abreast of the various computer programs used in advertising design and management.

EXPLORING

Read publications like *Advertising Age* (http://www.adage.com), *Adweek* (http://www.adweek.com), and *Brandweek* (http://www.brandweek.com) to become familiar with advertising issues, trends, successes, and failures. Visit the Clio Awards Web site (http://www.clioawards.com). Clios are given each year in a variety of categories, including television/cinema/digital, billboard, poster, radio, print/direct mail, interactive, and student work. The site also has information about advertising and art schools, trade associations, and links to some of the trade magazines of the industry.

To gain practical business experience, become involved with advertising or promotion activities at your school for social events, sports events, political issues, or fund-raising events. If your school newspaper or yearbook has paid advertising, offer to work in ad sales.

EMPLOYERS

Approximately 170,000 advertising account executives work in the United States. Advertising agencies all across the country and abroad employ advertising account executives. Of the 19,200 full-service agencies in the United States, the large firms located in Chicago, Los Angeles, and New York, tend to dominate the advertising industry. However, 68 percent of these organizations employ fewer than five people. These "small shops" offer employment opportunities for account executives with experience, talent, and flexibility.

STARTING OUT

Many people aspiring to the job of account executive participate in internships or begin as assistant executives, allowing them to work with clients, study the market, and follow up on client service. This work gives students a good sense of the rhythm of the job and the type of work required of account executives.

College graduates, with or without experience, can start their job search in their school's career services office. Staff there can set up interviews and help polish resumes.

The advertising arena is rich with opportunities. When looking for employment, you don't have to target agencies. Instead, search for jobs with large businesses that may employ advertising staff. If you want to work at an agency, you'll find the competition intense for jobs. Once hired, account executives often participate in special training programs that both initiate them and help them to succeed.

ADVANCEMENT

Since practical experience and a broad base of knowledge are often required of advertising account executives, many employees work their way up through the company, from assistant to account executive to account manager and finally to department head. In smaller agencies, where promotions depend on experience and leadership, advancement may occur slowly. In larger firms, management training programs are often required for advancement. Continuing education is occasionally offered to account executives in these firms, often through local colleges or special seminars provided by professional societies.

EARNINGS

According to the U.S. Department of Labor, advertising account executives earned salaries that ranged from less than $21,460 to $91,280 or more annually in 2006, with median annual earnings of approximately $42,750. In smaller agencies, the salary may be much lower ($20,000 or less), and in larger firms, it is often much higher (more than $150,000). Salary bonuses are common for account executives. Benefits typically include vacation and sick leave, health and life insurance, and a retirement plan.

WORK ENVIRONMENT

It is not uncommon for advertising account executives to work long hours, including evenings and weekends. Informal meetings with clients, for example, frequently take place after normal business hours. In addition, some travel may be required when clients are based in other cities or states or when account executives must attend industry conferences.

Advertising agencies are usually highly charged with energy and are both physically and psychologically exciting places to work. The account executive works with others as a team in a creative environment where a lot of ideas are exchanged among colleagues.

As deadlines are critical in advertising, it is important that account executives possess the ability to handle pressure and stress effectively. Patience and flexibility are also essential, as are organization and time management skills.

OUTLOOK

The growth of the advertising industry depends on the health of the economy. In a thriving economy, advertising budgets are large, consumers tend to respond to advertising campaigns, and new products and services that require promotion are increasingly developed. Although the economy has been weaker as of late, the U.S. Department of Labor still predicts that employment for advertising account executives will grow faster than the average for all occupations through 2016.

Opportunities for advertising account executives should be strong due to the growth of online advertising, cable channels, and other advertising mediums. Growth will also occur as a result of the increasing Hispanic population in the United States. Advertisers are creating specialized advertising and marketing campaigns to reach this growing demographic group.

Most opportunities for advertising account executives will be in larger cities, such as Chicago, Los Angeles, and New York, that enjoy a high concentration of business. Competition for these jobs, however, will be intense. The successful candidate will be a college graduate with a lot of creativity, strong communications skills, and extensive experience in the advertising industry. Those able to speak another language will have an edge because of the increasing supply of products and services offered in foreign markets.

FOR MORE INFORMATION

For profiles of advertising workers and career information, contact
Advertising Educational Foundation
220 East 42nd Street, Suite 3300
New York, NY 10017-5806
Tel: 212-986-8060
http://www.aef.com

The AAF combines the mutual interests of corporate advertisers, agencies, media companies, suppliers, and academia. Visit its Web site to learn more about internships, scholarships, and awards.
American Advertising Federation (AAF)
1101 Vermont Avenue, NW, Suite 500
Washington, DC 20005-6306
Tel: 800-999-2231
Email: aaf@aaf.org
http://www.aaf.org

For industry information, contact
American Association of Advertising Agencies
405 Lexington Avenue, 18th Floor
New York, NY 10174-1801
Tel: 212-682-2500
http://www.aaaa.org

For information on the practice, study, and teaching of marketing, contact
American Marketing Association
311 South Wacker Drive, Suite 5800
Chicago, IL 60606-6629
Tel: 800-AMA-1150
http://www.marketingpower.com

INTERVIEW

Dr. Janet Slater is the head of the Department of Advertising (http:// www.comm.uiuc.edu/advertising) at the University of Illinois in Urbana, Illinois. She discussed the field with the editors of Careers in Focus: Advertising and Marketing.

Q. Please tell us about your program and your background.

A. The Department of Advertising at the University of Illinois offers both a B.S. and M.S. in advertising. The undergraduate program is four years of study and the master's can be completed in one academic year.

I spent 25 years in the industry working on the agency side of the business. After realizing the need for advertising professionals in advertising education, I returned to school to receive a master's and a Ph.D. And have been teaching advertising since 1997.

Q. What is one thing that young people may not know about a career in advertising?

A. Every job in the business requires creativity. Many students believe the only creative element is in designing the advertisements themselves. But in fact the development of the strategy, the media plan, organizing the budget, planning the timing of the campaign—everything—requires a great deal of creativity. In today's media market, wherein everything carries an advertising message, it is often thought that the media planning area is one of the most exciting and creative.

Q. What types of students pursue study in your program?

A. Students who chose to pursue advertising at Illinois have a great sense of curiosity and come from various backgrounds. Many students come into the major uncertain as to what area of advertising they are truly interested in. It only takes a few courses for them to determine where they fit. All advertising students need to be great writers, good researchers, and be adaptive to any situation. This is a fascinating industry—fast paced and ever changing. But it can also be overwhelming. It is not a 9–5 job with the same activities every day.

Q. What advice would you offer advertising majors as they graduate and look for jobs?

A. Find your competitive edge. What makes you different from everyone else? Be able to package that edge in a portfolio of work—research, writing samples, concepts, anything that showcases your talent. Don't define yourself in terms of the job—media planner, art director, etc. Define yourself by the skills you have—strategic thinker, research oriented, idea person, problem solver, etc.

Q. What is the employment outlook for the field? How is the field of advertising changing?

A. The employment outlook is always good for talented people. The industry is changing all the time—new media, international growth, consumer research, etc. There is always room for those who are interested in digital media—both planning and implementation, strategists and researchers.

Advertising and Marketing Managers

OVERVIEW

Advertising and marketing managers plan, organize, direct, and coordinate the operations of advertising and marketing firms. They may oversee an entire company, a geographical territory of a company's operations, or a specific department within a company. There are approximately 214,000 advertising and marketing managers employed in the United States.

HISTORY

The advertising industry formally emerged in the 1840s, when newspaper-advertising solicitors began representing groups of newspapers. In 1865, a new system was introduced: buying newspaper space and dividing and selling it to advertisers at higher prices. Other forms of advertising also came onto the scene. By the early 1900s, for example, outdoor posters developed into the billboard form, and the merchants who used them were the principal advertisers. In 1922, radio station WEAF in New York City offered program time to advertisers. The use of television advertising began just before the end of World War II. Today, the Internet is catapulting the world of advertising into a whole new realm, allowing vendors not only to target and reach customers, but to interact with them as well.

The business discipline of marketing began to take shape as sellers realized

QUICK FACTS

School Subjects
Business
Computer science
Speech

Personal Skills
Helping/teaching
Leadership/management

Work Environment
Primarily indoors
One location with some
travel

Minimum Education Level
Bachelor's degree

Salary Range
$36,230 to $73,060 to
$109,030+ (advertising
managers)
$51,160 to $98,720 to
$136,710+ (marketing
managers)

Certification or Licensing
None available

Outlook
About as fast as the average

DOT
164

GOE
10.01.01

NOC
0611

O*NET-SOC
11-2011.00, 11-2021.00

that if a group of potential buyers could be found for a product, the product could be better designed to suit the needs of those buyers. Sellers also discovered the importance of identifying a group of buyers before starting an advertising campaign. By doing so, the producer could style the campaign to reach that specific group and would have a better chance of launching a successful product. Marketing, therefore, provided a service for both sides of the business world, the seller and the buyer.

As the need for advertising and marketing grew, companies specializing in product promotion and specialization were born. It is no surprise that the increasingly complex responsibilities involved in advertising and marketing products and services require managers to organize and run day-to-day office activities.

THE JOB

Advertising and marketing managers formulate policies and administer the advertising and marketing firm's operations. Managers may oversee the operations of an entire company, a geographical territory of a company's operations, or a specific department. Managers direct a company's or a department's daily activities within the context of the organization's overall plan. They implement organizational policies and goals. This may involve developing sales or promotional materials, analyzing the department's budgetary requirements, and hiring, training, and supervising staff. Advertising and marketing managers are often responsible for long-range planning for their company or department. This means setting goals for the organization and developing a workable plan for meeting those goals.

Advertising and marketing managers coordinate their department's activities with other departments. If the firm is privately owned, the owner may be the manager. In a large corporation, however, there will be a management structure above the advertising and marketing manager.

In companies that have several different locations, advertising and marketing managers may be assigned to oversee specific geographic areas. For example, a large ad firm with facilities all across the nation is likely to have a number of managers in charge of various territories. There might be a Midwest manager, Southwest manager, Southeast manager, Northeast manager, and Northwest manager. These managers are often called *regional* or *area managers*. Some advertising and marketing firms break their management territories up into even smaller sections, such as a single state or a part of a state. Managers overseeing these smaller segments are often called *district managers,* and typically report directly to an area or regional manager.

Advertising managers are responsible for coordinating the work of researchers, copywriters, artists, telemarketers, space buyers, time buyers, and other specialists. One type of advertising manager is the *account manager,* who represents the agency to its clients. (See the article, Advertising Account Executives, for more information.)

Managers working at large advertising agencies generally supervise a variety of accounts, while those working at smaller agencies usually only handle certain types of clients. For example, smaller firms may carry only financial accounts, hotels, book publishers, or industrial clients. Some managers work for agencies that are known for promoting packaged goods. Others work in retail and department store promotion.

In contrast, marketing managers work with their staff and other advertising professionals to determine how ads should look, where they should be placed, and when the advertising should begin. Managers must keep staff focused on a target audience when working on the promotion of a particular product or service. Managers must also carefully time the release of an ad. For example, launching an advertising campaign too early may create interest well before the product is available. In such cases, by the time the product is released, the public may no longer be interested.

The marketing manager must also oversee his or her department in developing a distribution plan for products. If a product is expected to sell well to a certain group, for example, then marketing professionals must decide how to deliver to members of that group based on when and where they shop.

Once markets are evaluated and merchandise is designed, the actual production begins. The job of the manager is not yet done, however. Along with the public relations department, marketing managers contact members of the press with the aim of getting product information out to the public.

Because research studies show how a product looks on the shelf can often affect sales, managers work with designers to explore new color combinations, more appealing shapes, interesting patterns, and new materials.

Marketing managers use a scientific and statistical approach in answering a client's questions about selling a product to the public. The advertising aspect of a marketing campaign must get attention, arouse interest, secure belief, create desire, and stir action. Beauty, comfort, convenience, and quality are the promises that sell all kinds of products, from consumables to cars.

Managers discuss strategy for a new marketing campaign. *(C. Devan, zefa/Corbis)*

REQUIREMENTS

High School

The educational background of advertising and marketing managers varies as widely as the nature of their diverse responsibilities. If you are interested in a managerial career, you should start preparing in high school by taking college preparatory classes. Because strong communication skills are important, take as many English classes as possible. Speech classes are another way to improve your communication skills. Courses in business, computer science, economics, and mathematics are also excellent choices to help you prepare for this career.

Postsecondary Training

Most advertising and marketing managers have a bachelor's degree in advertising, marketing, or business administration. However, degrees in economics, English, the fine arts, journalism, or speech communications are also applicable. Useful college classes include those in business, economics, psychology, sociology, and any art medium. Graduate and professional degrees are common at the managerial level.

Advertising and Marketing Glossaries

About.com: Marketing
http://marketing.about.com/od/marketingglossary/a/marketing
terms.htm

Advertising Glossary
http://www.advertisingglossary.net

American Marketing Association
http://www.marketingpower.com/mg-dictionary.php

Google Advertising
http://www.google.com/ads/glossary.html

University of Texas at Austin: Department of Advertising
http://advertising.utexas.edu/research/terms

Because managers coordinate the efforts of their whole departments, most have worked in other lower-level advertising and marketing jobs. Candidates for managerial positions who have extensive experience and developed portfolios will have a competitive edge.

Other Requirements

There are a number of personal characteristics that advertising and marketing managers need to succeed in their work. You will need good communication and interpersonal skills and the ability to delegate work to other members of your staff. Because advertising and marketing campaigns are often run under strict deadlines, the ability to think on your feet and work well under pressure is critical.

Other traits considered important for advertising and marketing managers are intelligence, decisiveness, intuition, creativity, honesty, loyalty, a sense of responsibility, and planning abilities.

EXPLORING

To get experience in this line of work, try developing your own ad campaign. Take a product you enjoy, for example, a brand of soda you drink, and try to organize a written ad campaign. Consider the type of customers you should target and what wording and images would work best to attract this audience.

You can also explore this career by developing your managerial skills in general. Whether you're involved in drama, sports, school publications, or a part-time job, there are managerial duties associated with any organized activity. These can involve planning, scheduling, managing other workers or volunteers, fund-raising, or budgeting.

EMPLOYERS

Approximately 47,000 advertising and promotions managers and 167,000 marketing managers are employed in the United States. Nearly 25 percent of all advertising and promotions managers work in professional, scientific, and technical services industries and the wholesale trade industry.

Virtually every business in the United States has some form of advertising and marketing position. Obviously, the larger the company is, the more managerial positions it is likely to have. Another factor is the geographical territory covered by the business. Companies doing business in larger geographical territories are apt to have more managerial positions than those with smaller territories.

STARTING OUT

You will first need experience in lower-level advertising and marketing jobs before advancing to a managerial position. To break into an advertising or marketing firm, use your college career services office for assistance. In addition, a number of firms advertise job listings in newspapers and Internet job boards.

Your first few jobs in advertising and marketing should give you experience in working with clients, studying the market, and following up on client service. This work will give you a good sense of the rhythm of the job and the type of work required.

ADVANCEMENT

Most advertising and marketing management and top executive positions are filled by experienced lower-level workers who have displayed valuable skills, such as leadership, self-confidence, creativity, motivation, decisiveness, and flexibility. In smaller firms, advancement to a management position may come slowly, while promotions may occur more quickly in larger firms.

Promotion may be accelerated by participating in advanced training programs sponsored by industry and trade associations or by enrolling in continuing education programs at local universities. These programs are sometimes paid for by the firm. Managers committed to improving their knowledge of the field and of related disciplines—especially computer information systems—will have the best opportunities for advancement.

EARNINGS

The median annual earnings for advertising and promotions managers were $73,060 in 2006, according to the U.S. Department of Labor. The lowest 10 percent earned $36,230 or less, while the highest 25 percent earned $109,030 or more. The median salary for marketing managers was $98,720. The lowest 10 percent earned $51,160 or less, while the highest 25 percent earned $136,710 or more.

Salary levels vary substantially, depending on the level of responsibility, length of service, and type, size, and location of the advertising and marketing firm. Top-level managers in large firms can earn much more than their counterparts in small firms. Also, salaries in large metropolitan areas, such as New York City, are higher than those in smaller cities.

Benefit and compensation packages for managers are usually excellent, and may even include bonuses, stock awards, and company-paid insurance premiums.

WORK ENVIRONMENT

Advertising and marketing managers are provided with comfortable offices near the departments they direct. Higher-level managers may have spacious, lavish offices and may enjoy such privileges as executive dining rooms, company cars, country club memberships, and liberal expense accounts.

Managers often work long hours under intense pressure to meet advertising and marketing goals. Workweeks consisting of 55 to 60 hours at the office are not uncommon—in fact, some higher-level managers spend up to 80 hours working each week. These long hours limit time available for family and leisure activities.

Advertising and marketing firms are usually highly charged with energy and are both physically and psychologically exciting places to work. Managers work with others as a team in a creative environment where a lot of ideas are exchanged among colleagues. As deadlines are critical in marketing and advertising campaigns, it is important that the manager possesses the ability to handle pressure and stress effectively. Patience and flexibility are also essential, as are organization and time management skills.

OUTLOOK

Overall, employment of advertising and marketing managers and executives is expected to grow about as fast as the average for all occupations through 2016, according to the U.S. Department of Labor. Many job openings will be the result of managers being promoted to better positions, retiring, or leaving their positions to start their own businesses. Others will be created as a result of increased advertising and marketing on television, radio, and in outdoor advertising. Even so, the compensation and prestige of these positions make them highly sought after, and competition to fill openings will be intense. College graduates with experience, a high level of creativity, and strong communication skills should have the best job opportunities.

The outlook for the advertising and marketing industries is closely tied to the overall economy. When the economy is good, business expands both in terms of the firm's output and the number of people it employs, which creates a need for more managers. In economic downturns, firms often lay off employees and cut back on production, which lessens the need for managers.

FOR MORE INFORMATION

For profiles of advertising workers and career information, contact
Advertising Educational Foundation
220 East 42nd Street, Suite 3300
New York, NY 10017-5806
Tel: 212-986-8060
http://www.aef.com

The AAF combines the mutual interests of corporate advertisers, agencies, media companies, suppliers, and academia. Visit its Web site to learn more about internships, scholarships, student chapters, and awards.
American Advertising Federation (AAF)
1101 Vermont Avenue, NW, Suite 500
Washington, DC 20005-6306
Tel: 800-999-2231
Email: aaf@aaf.org
http://www.aaf.org

For industry information, contact
American Association of Advertising Agencies
405 Lexington Avenue, 18th Floor
New York, NY 10174-1801
Tel: 212-682-2500
http://www.aaaa.org

For information on the practice, study, and teaching of marketing, contact
American Marketing Association
311 South Wacker Drive, Suite 5800
Chicago, IL 60606-6629

Tel: 800-262-1150
http://www.marketingpower.com

For a brochure on a career in management, contact
National Management Association
2210 Arbor Boulevard
Dayton, OH 45439-1506
Tel: 937-294-0421
Email: nma@nma1.org
http://nma1.org

Advertising Workers

OVERVIEW

Advertising is defined as mass communication paid for by an advertiser to persuade a particular segment of the public to adopt ideas or take actions of benefit to the advertiser. *Advertising workers* perform the various creative and business activities needed to take an advertisement from the research stage, to creative concept, through production, and finally to its intended audience. There are more than 170,000 advertising sales agents and 47,000 advertising and promotions managers employed in the United States.

HISTORY

Advertising has been around as long as people have been exchanging goods and services. While a number of innovations spurred the development of advertising, it wasn't until the invention of the printing press in the 15th century that merchants began posting handbills to advertise their goods and services. By the 19th century, newspapers became an important means of advertising, followed by magazines in the late 1800s.

One of the problems confronting merchants in the early days of advertising was where to place their ads to generate the most business. In response, a number of people emerged who specialized in the area of advertising, accepting ads and posting them conspicuously. These agents were the first advertising workers. As competition among merchants increased, many of these agents offered to compose ads, as well as post them, for their clients.

Today, with intense competition among both new and existing businesses, advertising has become a necessity in the marketing of goods and services alike. At the same time, the advertising worker's job has grown more demanding and complex than ever. With a wide variety of media from which advertisers can choose—including newspapers, magazines, billboards, radio, television, film and video, the World Wide Web, and a variety of other new technologies—today's advertising worker must not only develop and create ads and campaigns, but keep abreast of current and developing buying and technology trends as well.

THE JOB

Approximately four out of every 10 advertising organizations in the United States are full-service operations, offering their clients a broad range of services, including copywriting, graphics and other art-related work, production, media placement, and tracking and follow-up. These advertising agencies may have hundreds of people working in a dozen different departments, while smaller companies often employ just a handful of workers. Most agencies, however, have at least five departments: contact, research, media, creative, and production.

Contact department personnel are responsible for attracting new customers and maintaining relationships with existing ones. Heading the contact department, *advertising agency managers* are concerned with the overall activities of the company. They formulate plans to generate business by either soliciting new accounts or getting additional business from established clients. In addition, they meet with department heads to coordinate their operations and to create policies and procedures.

Advertising account executives are the employees responsible for maintaining good relations between their clients and the agency. Acting as liaisons, they represent the agency to its clients and must therefore be able to communicate clearly and effectively. After examining the advertising objectives of their clients, account executives develop campaigns or strategies and then work with others from the various agency departments to target specific audiences, create advertising communications, and execute the campaigns. Presenting concepts, as well as the ad campaign at various stages of completion, to clients for their feedback and approval, account executives must have some knowledge of overall marketing strategies and be able to sell ideas. For more information on this career, see the article Advertising Account Executives.

Working with account executives, employees in the research department gather, analyze, and interpret the information needed to make a client's advertising campaign successful. By determining who the potential buyers of a product or service will be, *research workers* predict which theme will have the most impact, what kind of packaging and price will have the most appeal, and which media will be the most effective.

Guided by a *research director,* research workers conduct local, regional, and national surveys to examine consumer preferences and then determine potential sales for the targeted product or service based on those preferences. Researchers also gather information about competitors' products, prices, sales, and advertising methods. To learn what the buying public prefers in a client's product over a competitor's, research workers often distribute samples and then ask the users of these samples for their opinions of the product. This information can then be used as testimonials about the product or as a means of identifying the most persuasive selling message in an ad.

Although research workers often recommend which media to use for an advertising campaign, *media planners* are the specialists who determine which print or broadcast media will be the most effective. Ultimately, they are responsible for choosing the combination of media that will reach the greatest number of potential buyers for the least amount of money, based on their clients' advertising strategies. Accordingly, planners must be familiar with the markets that each medium reaches, as well as the advantages and disadvantages of advertising in each. For more information on this career, see the article Media Planners and Buyers.

Media buyers, often referred to as *space buyers* (for newspapers and magazines), or *time buyers* (for radio and television), do the actual purchasing of space and time according to a general plan formulated by the media director. In addition to ensuring that ads appear when and where they should, buyers negotiate costs for ad placement and maintain contact and extensive correspondence with clients and media representatives alike. For more information on this career, see the article Media Planners and Buyers.

While the contact, research, and media departments handle the business side of a client's advertising campaign, the creative staff takes care of the artistic aspects. *Creative directors* oversee the activities of artists and writers and work with clients and account executives to determine the best advertising approaches, gain approval on concepts, and establish budgets and schedules.

Copywriters take the ideas submitted by creative directors and account executives and write descriptive text in the form of headlines, jingles, slogans, and other copy designed to attract the attention of potential buyers. In addition to being able to express themselves clearly and persuasively, copywriters must know what motivates people to buy. They must also be able to describe a product's features in a captivating and appealing way and be familiar

Advertising workers must be able to work well with others. Above, two advertising workers discuss the details of an advertising campaign. *(Kim Eriksen, zefa/Corbis)*

with various advertising media. In large agencies, copywriters may be supervised by a copy chief. For more information on this career, see the article Copywriters.

Copywriters work closely with *art directors* to make sure that text and artwork create a unified, eye-catching arrangement. Planning the visual presentation of the client's message, from concept formulation to final artwork, the art director plays an important role in every stage of the creation of an advertising campaign. Art directors who work on filmed commercials and videos combine film techniques, music, and sound, as well as actors or animation, to communicate an advertiser's message. In publishing, art directors work with graphic designers, photographers, copywriters, and editors to develop brochures, catalogs, direct mail, and other printed pieces, all according to the advertising strategy.

Art directors must have a basic knowledge of graphics and design, computer software, printing, photography, and filmmaking. With the help of *graphic artists*, they decide where to place text and images, choose typefaces, and create storyboard ads and videos. Several layouts are usually submitted to the client, who chooses one or asks for revisions until a layout or conceptualization sketch meets with final approval. The art director then selects an illustrator, graphic artist, photographer, or TV or video producer, and the project moves on to the production department of the agency. For more information on these careers, see the articles Art Directors and Graphic Designers.

Production departments in large ad agencies may be divided into print production and broadcast production divisions, each with its own managers and staff. *Production managers* and their assistants convert and reproduce written copy and artwork into printed, filmed, or tape-recorded form so that they can be presented to the public. Production employees work closely with imaging, printing, engraving, and other art reproduction firms and must be familiar with various printing processes, papers, inks, typography, still and motion picture photography, digital imaging, and other processes and materials.

In addition to the principal employees in the five major departments, advertising organizations work with a variety of staff or freelancers who have specialized knowledge, education, and skill, including photographers, photoengravers, typographers, printers, telemarketers, product and package designers, and producers of display materials. Finally, rounding out most advertising establishments are various support employees, such as production coordinators, video editors, word processors, statisticians, accountants, administrators, secretaries, and clerks.

The work of advertising employees is fast paced, dynamic, and ever changing, depending on each client's strategies and budgets and the creative ideas generated by agency workers. In addition to innovative techniques, methods, media, and materials used by agency workers, new and emerging technologies are impacting the work of everyone in the advertising arena, from marketing executives to graphic designers. The Internet is undoubtedly the most revolutionary medium to hit the advertising scene. Through this worldwide, computer-based network, researchers are able to precisely target markets and clearly identify consumer needs. In addition, the Internet's Web pages provide media specialists with a powerful vehicle for advertising their clients' products and services. New technology has also been playing an important role in the creative area. Most art directors, for example, use a variety of computer software programs, and many create and oversee Web sites for their clients. Other interactive materials and vehicles, such as CD catalogs, touch-screens, multidimensional visuals, and voice-mail shopping, are changing the way today's advertising workers are doing their jobs.

REQUIREMENTS

High School

You can prepare for a career as an advertising worker by taking a variety of courses in high school. General liberal arts courses, such as business, communications, economics, English, journalism, mathematics, psychology, social science, and speech, are important for aspiring advertising employees. In addition, those interested in the creative side of the field should take such classes as art, art history, drawing, graphic design, and illustration. Finally, since computers play a vital role in the advertising field, you should become familiar with word processing and layout programs, as well as the World Wide Web.

Postsecondary Training

The American Association of Advertising Agencies notes that most agencies employing entry-level personnel prefer college graduates. (In 2006, approximately 62 percent of advertising sales agents had at least an associate's degree, according to the U.S. Department of Labor.) Copywriters are best prepared with a college degree in com-

Top Advertising Programs

Most Mentions by College Faculty as a "Top 3" Undergraduate
Program
   1. University of Texas (http://advertising.utexas.edu/programs)
   2. Michigan State University (http://adv.msu.edu)
   3. University of Illinois (http://www.comm.uiuc.edu/advertising)

Most Mentions by College Faculty as a "Top 3" Graduate Program
   1. University of Texas (http://advertising.utexas.edu/programs)
   2. Northwestern University (http://www.northwestern.edu)
   3. University of Illinois (http://www.comm.uiuc.edu/advertising)
   3. Michigan State University (http://adv.msu.edu)

Source: University of Texas at Austin

munications, English, or journalism; research workers need college training in market research, social studies, and statistics; and most account executives have business or related degrees. Media positions are increasingly requiring a college degree in communications or a technology-related area. Media directors and research directors with a master's degree have a distinct advantage over those with only an undergraduate degree. Some research department heads even have doctorates.

While the requirements from agency to agency may vary somewhat, graduates of liberal arts colleges or those with majors in fields such as business administration, communications, journalism, or marketing research are preferred. Good language skills, as well as a broad liberal arts background, are necessary for advertising workers. College students interested in the field should take such courses as advertising, art, economics, English, foreign languages, marketing, mathematics, philosophy, psychology, social studies, sociology, statistics, and writing. Some 900 degree-granting institutions throughout the United States offer specialized majors in advertising as part of their curriculum.

Other Requirements
In addition to the variety of educational and work experiences necessary for those aspiring to advertising careers, many personal characteristics are also important. Although you will perform

many tasks of your job independently as an advertising worker, you will also interact with others as part of a team. Moreover, you may be responsible for initiating and maintaining client contact. You must therefore be able to get along well with people and communicate clearly.

Advertising is not a job that involves routine, and you must be able to meet and adjust to the challenges presented by each new client and product or service. The ability to think clearly and logically is important, because commonsense approaches rather than gimmicks persuade people that something is worth buying. You must also be creative, flexible, and imaginative in order to anticipate consumer demand and trends, to develop effective concepts, and to sell the ideas, products, and services of your clients.

Finally, with technology evolving at breakneck speed, it's vital that you keep pace with technological advances and trends. Besides being able to work with the most current software and hardware, you should be familiar with the Web, as well as with other technology that is impacting—and will continue to impact—the industry.

EXPLORING

If you aspire to a career in the advertising industry, you can gain valuable insight by taking writing and art courses offered either in school or by private organizations. In addition to the theoretical ideas and techniques that such classes provide, you can actually apply what you learn by working full or part time at local department stores or newspaper offices. Some advertising agencies or research firms also employ students to interview people or to conduct other market research. Work as an agency clerk or messenger may also be available. Participating in internships at an advertising or marketing organization is yet another way to explore the field, as well as to determine your aptitude for advertising work. You may find it helpful to read publications dedicated to this industry, such as *Advertising Age* (http://www.adage.com).

EMPLOYERS

More than 170,000 advertising sales agents and 47,000 advertising and promotions managers are employed in the United States. Most advertising workers are employed by advertising agencies that plan and prepare advertising material for their clients on a commission or service-fee basis. However, some large companies and nearly all department stores prefer to handle their own advertising. Advertising workers in such organizations prepare advertising materials for in-house clients, such as the marketing or catalog department. They also may be involved in the planning, preparation, and production of special promotional materials, such as sales brochures, articles describing the activities of the organization, or Web sites. Some advertising workers are employed by owners of various media, including newspapers, magazines, radio and television networks, and outdoor advertising. Workers employed in these media are mainly sales representatives who sell advertising space or broadcast time to advertising agencies or companies that maintain their own advertising departments.

Besides agencies, large companies, and department stores, advertising services and supply houses employ such advertising specialists as photographers, photoengravers, typographers, printers, product and package designers, display producers, and others who assist in the production of various advertising materials.

Of the 19,200 advertising agencies in the United States, most of the large firms are located in Chicago, Los Angeles, and New York. Employment opportunities are also available, however, at a variety of "small shops," 68 percent of which employ fewer than five workers each. A growing number of self-employment and home-based business opportunities are resulting in a variety of industry jobs located in outlying areas rather than in big cities.

STARTING OUT

Although competition for advertising jobs is fierce and getting your foot in the door can be difficult, there are a variety of ways to launch a career in the field. Some large advertising agencies recruit college graduates and place them in training programs designed to acquaint beginners with all aspects of advertising work, but these opportunities are limited and highly competitive.

Instead, many graduates simply send resumes to businesses that employ entry-level advertising workers. Newspapers, radio and television stations, printers, photographers, and advertising agencies are but a few of the businesses that will hire beginners. *The Standard Directory of Advertising Agencies* (New Providence, N.J.: National Register Publishing Company, 2003) lists the names and addresses of ad agencies all across the nation. You can find the directory in almost any public library.

Those who have had work experience in sales positions often enter the advertising field as account executives. High school graduates and other people without experience who want to work in advertising, however, may find it necessary to begin as clerks or assistants to research and production staff members or to copywriters.

ADVANCEMENT

The career path in an advertising agency generally leads from trainee to skilled worker to division head and then to department head. It may also take employees from department to department, allowing them to gain more responsibility with each move. Opportunities abound for those with talent, leadership capability, and ambition.

Management positions require experience in all aspects of advertising, including agency work, communication with advertisers, and knowledge of various advertising media. Copywriters, account executives, and other advertising agency workers who demonstrate outstanding ability to deal with clients and supervise coworkers usually have a good chance of advancing to management positions. Other workers, however, prefer to acquire specialized skills. For them, advancement may mean more responsibility, the opportunity to perform more specialized tasks, and increased pay.

Advertising workers at various department stores, mail order houses, and other large firms that have their own advertising departments can also earn promotions. Advancement in any phase of advertising work is usually dependent on the employee's experience, training, and demonstrated skills.

Some qualified copywriters, artists, and account executives establish their own agencies or become marketing consultants. For these entrepreneurs, advancement may take the form of an increasing number of accounts and/or more prestigious clients.

EARNINGS

Salaries of advertising workers vary depending on the type of work, the size of the agency, its geographic location, the kind of accounts handled, and the agency's gross earnings. Salaries are also determined by a worker's education, aptitude, and experience. The wide range of jobs in advertising makes it difficult to estimate average salaries for all positions.

The U.S. Department of Labor (USDL) reports that the average annual earnings for advertising and promotions managers were $73,060 in 2006. For marketing managers the average was $98,720, sales managers earned $91,560, and public relations managers made $82,180 per year. The lowest paid 10 percent of advertising and promotions managers averaged less than $36,230, while the highest paid earned more than $109,030.

The USDL reports that the mean annual earnings for advertising sales agents were $42,750 in 2006. The lowest paid 10 percent of all advertising sales agents earned less than $21,460, while the highest paid advertising sales agents earned more than $91,280.

In advertising agencies, chief executives can earn from $100,000 annually upward to $750,000. In the research and media departments, research directors average $75,000 annually; experienced analysts, up to $75,000 per year; media directors, between $50,000 and $100,000 annually; and media planners and buyers, $25,000 to $130,000 per year. In the creative department, art directors earn between $37,000 and $135,000 or more annually; and creative directors, $50,000 to $100,000 per year. Finally, production managers make about $45,000 per year.

In other businesses and industries, individual earnings vary widely. Salaries of advertising workers are generally higher, however, at consumer product firms than at industrial product organizations because of the competition among consumer product producers. The majority of companies offer insurance benefits, a retirement plan, and other incentives and bonuses.

WORK ENVIRONMENT

Conditions at most agencies are similar to those found in other offices throughout the country, except that employees must frequently work under great pressure to meet deadlines. While a traditional 40-hour workweek is the norm at some companies, many full-time employees report that they work more than 40 hours per week, including evenings and weekends. Bonuses and time off during slow periods are sometimes provided as a means of compensation for unusual workloads and hours.

Although some advertising employees, such as researchers, work independently on a great many tasks, most must function as part of a team. With frequent meetings with coworkers, clients, and media representatives alike, the work environment is usually energized, with ideas being exchanged, contracts being negotiated, and schedules being modified.

Advertising work is fast paced and exciting. As a result, many employees often feel stressed as they are constantly challenged to take initiative and be creative. Nevertheless, advertising workers enjoy both professional and personal satisfaction in seeing the culmination of their work communicated to sometimes millions of people.

OUTLOOK

Employment for advertising sales workers is expected to grow faster than the average for all occupations through 2016, according to the U.S. Department of Labor. Network and cable television, radio, newspapers, the Web, and certain other media (particularly interactive vehicles) will offer advertising workers an increasing number of employment opportunities. Some media, such as magazines, direct mail, and event marketing, are expected to provide fewer job opportunities.

Advertising agencies will enjoy faster than average employment growth, as will industries that service ad agencies and other businesses in the advertising field, such as those that offer commercial photography, imaging, art, and graphics services.

At the two extremes, enormous "mega-agencies" and small shops employing up to only 10 workers each offer employment opportunities for people with experience, talent, flexibility, and drive. In addition, self-employment and home-based businesses are on the rise. Many nonindustrial companies, such as banks, schools, and hospitals, will also be creating advertising positions.

In general, openings will become available to replace workers who change positions, retire, or leave the field for other reasons. Competition for these jobs will be keen, however, because of the large number of qualified professionals in this traditionally desirable field. Opportunities will be best for the well-qualified and well-trained applicant. Employers favor college graduates with experience, a high level of creativity, and strong communications skills. People who are not well qualified or prepared for agency work will find the advertising field increasingly difficult to enter. The same is also true for those who seek work in companies that service ad agencies.

FOR MORE INFORMATION

For information on student chapters, scholarships, and internships, contact
American Advertising Federation
1101 Vermont Avenue, NW, Suite 500
Washington, DC 20005-6306

Tel: 800-999-2231
Email: aaf@aaf.org
http://www.aaf.org

For profiles of advertising workers and career information, contact
Advertising Educational Foundation
220 East 42nd Street, Suite 3300
New York, NY 10017-5806
Tel: 212-986-8060
http://www.aded.org

For industry information, contact
American Association of Advertising Agencies
405 Lexington, 18th Floor
New York, NY 10174-1801
Tel: 212-682-2500
http://www.aaaa.org

For career and salary information, contact
American Marketing Association
311 South Wacker Drive, Suite 5800
Chicago, IL 60606-6629
Tel: 800-AMA-1150
http://www.marketingpower.com

*The Art Directors Club is an international, nonprofit organization
for creative professionals in advertising, graphic design, interactive
media, broadcast design, typography, packaging, environmental
design, photography, illustration, and related disciplines.*
The Art Directors Club
106 West 29th Street
New York, NY 10001-5301
Tel: 212-643-1440
Email: info@adcny.org
http://www.adcglobal.org

For information on student membership and careers, contact
Direct Marketing Association
1120 Avenue of the Americas
New York, NY 10036-6700
Tel: 212-768-7277
http://www.the-dma.org

The Graphic Artists Guild promotes and protects the economic interests of the artist/designer and is committed to improving conditions for all creators of graphic art and raising standards for the entire industry.

Graphic Artists Guild
32 Broadway, Suite 1114
New York, NY 10004-1612
Tel: 212-791-3400
http://www.gag.org

Art Directors

OVERVIEW

Art directors play a key role in every stage of an advertisement or ad campaign, from formulating concepts to supervising production. Ultimately, they are responsible for planning and overseeing the presentation of their clients' messages in print or on screen—that is, in books, magazines, newspapers, television commercials, posters, and packaging, as well as in film and video and on the Internet.

In publishing, art directors work with artists, photographers, and text editors to develop visual images and generate copy according to the marketing strategy. They evaluate existing illustrations, determine presentation styles and techniques, hire both staff and freelance talent, work with layouts, and prepare budgets.

In films, videos, and television commercials, art directors set the general look of the visual elements and approve the props, costumes, and models. In addition, they are involved in casting, editing, and selecting the music. In film (motion pictures) and video, the art director is usually an experienced animator or computer/graphic arts designer who supervises animators or other artistic staff.

In sum, art directors are charged with selling to, informing, and educating consumers. They supervise both in-house and off-site staff, handle executive issues, and oversee the entire artistic production process. There are approximately 10,000 art directors employed in the advertising industry in the United States.

QUICK FACTS

School Subjects
Art
Business
Computer science

Personal Skills
Artistic
Communication/ideas

Work Environment
Primarily indoors
Primarily one location

Minimum Education Level
Bachelor's degree

Salary Range
$37,920 to $82,680 to $135,090+

Certification or Licensing
None available

Outlook
About as fast as the average

DOT
164

GOE
01.01.01

NOC
5131

O*NET-SOC
27-1011.00

HISTORY

Artists have been an important part of the creative process throughout history. Medieval monks illuminated their manuscripts, painting with egg-white tempera on vellum. Each copy of each book had to be printed and illustrated individually.

Printed illustrations first appeared in books in 1461. Through the years, prints were made through woodblock, copperplate, lithography, and other means of duplicating images. Although making many copies of the same illustration was now possible, publishers still depended on individual artists to create the original works. Text editors usually decided what was to be illustrated and how, while artists commonly supervised the production of the artwork.

The first art directors were probably staff illustrators for book publishers. As the publishing industry grew more complex and incorporated new technologies such as photography and film, art direction evolved into a more supervisory position and became a full-time job. Publishers and advertisers began to need specialists who could acquire and use illustrations and photos. Women's magazines, such as *Vogue* (http://www.style.com/vogue) and *Harper's Bazaar* (http://www.harpersbazaar.com), and photo magazines, such as *National Geographic* (http://www.nationalgeographic.com), relied so heavily on illustration and photography that the photo editor and art director began to carry as much power as the text editor.

With the creation of animation, art directors became more indispensable than ever. Animated short films, such as the early Mickey Mouse cartoons, were usually supervised by art directors. Walt Disney, himself, was the art director on many of his early pictures. And as full-length films have moved into animation, the sheer number of illustrations requires more than one art director to oversee the project.

Today's art directors supervise almost every type of visual project produced. Through a variety of methods and media, from television and film to magazines, comic books, and the Internet, art directors communicate ideas by selecting and supervising every element that goes into the finished product.

THE JOB

Art directors are responsible for all visual aspects of printed or on-screen projects. The art director oversees the process of developing visual solutions to a variety of communication problems. He or she helps to establish corporate identities; advertises products and services; enhances books, magazines, newsletters, and other publications; and creates television commercials, film and video productions, and Web sites. Some art directors with experience or knowledge in specific fields specialize in such areas as packaging, exhibitions and displays, or the Internet. But all directors, even those with specialized backgrounds, must be skilled in and knowledgeable about design, illustration, photography, computers, research, and writing to supervise the work of graphic artists, photographers, copywriters, text editors, and other employees.

In print advertising and publishing, art directors may begin with the client's concept or develop one in collaboration with the copywriter and account executive. Once the concept is established, the next step is to decide on the most effective way to communicate it. If there is text, for example, should the art director choose illustrations based on specific text references, or should the illustrations fill in the gaps in the copy? If a piece is being revised, existing illustrations must be reevaluated.

After deciding what needs to be illustrated, art directors must find sources that can create or provide the art. Photo agencies, for example, have photographs and illustrations on thousands of different subjects. If, however, the desired illustration does not exist, it may have to be commissioned or designed by one of the staff designers. Commissioning artwork means that the art director contacts a photographer or illustrator and explains what is needed. A price is negotiated, and the artist creates the image specifically for the art director.

Once the illustrations and other art elements have been secured, they must be presented in an appealing manner. The art director supervises (and may help in the production of) the layout and presents the final version of the piece to the client or creative director. Layout is the process of figuring out where every image, headline, and block of text will be placed on the page. The size, style, and method of reproduction must all be specifically indicated so that the image is recreated as the director intended it.

In broadcast advertising and film and video, the art director has a wide variety of responsibilities and often interacts with an enormous number of creative professionals. Working with directors and producers, art directors interpret scripts and create or select settings to visually convey the story or the message. The art director oversees and channels the talents of set decorators and designers, model makers, location managers, propmasters, construction coordinators, and special effects people. In addition, art directors work with writers, unit production managers, cinematographers, costume designers, and post-production staff, including editors and employees responsible for scoring and titles. The art director is ultimately responsible for all visual aspects of the finished product.

The process of producing a television commercial begins in much the same way that a printed advertising piece is created. The art director may start with the client's concept or create one in-house in collaboration with staff members. Once a concept has been created and the copywriter has generated the corresponding text, the art director sketches a rough storyboard based on the writer's ideas, and the plan is presented for review to the creative director. The next step is to develop a finished storyboard, with larger and more detailed frames (the individual scenes) in color. This storyboard is presented to the client for review and used as a guide for the film director as well.

Technology has been playing an increasingly important role in the art director's job. Most art directors, for example, use a variety of computer software programs, including Adobe InDesign, Frame-Maker, Illustrator, and Photoshop; Macromedia Dreamweaver; QuarkXPress; and CorelDRAW. Many others create and oversee Web sites for clients and work with other interactive media and materials, including CD-ROM, touch-screens, multidimensional visuals, and new animation programs.

Art directors usually work on more than one project at a time and must be able to keep numerous, unrelated details straight. They often work under pressure of a deadline and yet must remain calm and pleasant when dealing with clients and staff. Because they are supervisors, art directors are often called on to resolve problems, not only with projects but with employees as well.

Art directors are not entry-level workers. They usually have years of experience working at lower-level jobs in the field before gaining the knowledge needed to supervise projects. Depending on whether they work primarily in publishing or film, art directors have to know how printing presses operate or how film is processed. They should also be familiar with a variety of production techniques to understand the wide range of ways that images can be manipulated to meet the needs of a project.

REQUIREMENTS

High School

A college degree is usually a requirement for art directors; however, in some instances, it is not absolutely necessary. A variety of high school courses will give you both a taste of college-level offerings and an idea of the skills necessary for art directors on the job. These courses include advertising, art, art history, desktop publishing, drawing, graphic design, illustration, and photography.

Math courses are also important. Most of the elements of sizing an image involve calculating percentage reduction or enlargement of the original picture. This must be done with a great degree of accuracy if the overall design is going to work. For example, type size may have to be figured within a thirty-second of an inch for a print project. Errors can be extremely costly and may make the project look sloppy.

Other useful courses that you should take in high school include business, computing, cultural studies, English, psychology, social science, and technical drawing.

Postsecondary Training

According to the American Institute of Graphic Arts, nine out of 10 artists have a college degree. Among them, six out of 10 have majored in graphic design, and two out of 10 have majored in fine arts. In addition, almost two out of 10 have a master's degree. Along with general two- and four-year colleges and universities, a number of professional art schools offer two-, three-, or four-year programs with such classes as figure drawing, graphic design, and painting, as well as classes in art history, business administration, communications, foreign languages, and writing.

Courses in advertising, desktop publishing, fashion, filmmaking, layout, marketing, photography, and set direction are also important for those interested in becoming art directors. Specialized courses, sometimes offered only at professional art schools, may be particularly helpful for students who want to go into art direction. These include animation, portfolio development, storyboard, typography, and Web site design.

Because of the rapidly increasing use of computers in design work, it is essential to have a thorough understanding of how computer art and layout programs work. In smaller companies, the art director may be responsible for operating this equipment; in larger companies, a staff person, under the direction of the art director, may use these programs. In either case, the director must know what can be done with the available equipment.

In addition to course work at the college level, many universities and professional art schools offer graduates or students in their final year a variety of workshop projects, desktop publishing training opportunities, and internships. These programs provide students with opportunities to develop their personal design styles as well as their portfolios.

Other Requirements

The work of an art director requires creativity, imagination, curiosity, and a sense of adventure. Art directors must be able to work with all sorts of specialized equipment and computer software, such as graphic design programs, as well as make presentations on the ideas behind their work.

The ability to work well with different people and organizations is a must for art directors. They must always be up to date on new techniques, trends, and attitudes. And because deadlines are a constant part of the work, an ability to handle stress and pressure well is key.

Accuracy and attention to detail are important parts of the job. When art is done neatly and correctly, the public usually pays no notice. But when a project is done poorly or sloppily, people will notice, even if they have had no design training. Other requirements for art directors include time management skills and an interest in media and people's motivations and lifestyles.

EXPLORING

High school students can get an idea of what an art director does by working on the staff of the school newspaper, magazine, or yearbook, and developing their own Web sites or zines. It may also be possible to secure a part-time job assisting the advertising director of the local newspaper or to work at an advertising agency. Developing your own artistic talent is important, and this can be accomplished through self-training (reading books and practicing) or through courses in painting, drawing, or other creative arts. At the very least, you should develop your "creative eye"—that is, your ability to develop ideas visually. One way to do this is by familiarizing yourself with great works, such as paintings or highly creative magazine ads, motion pictures, videos, or commercials.

Students can also become members of a variety of art or advertising clubs around the nation. If you have access to the Internet, check out Paleta: The Art Project (http://www.paletaworld.org) to join a free art club. In addition to keeping members up to date on industry trends, such clubs offer job information, resources, and a variety of other benefits.

EMPLOYERS

Approximately 10,000 art directors work in the advertising industry (the largest employer of these professionals). Additionally, a variety of organizations in virtually all industries employ art directors. They might work at publishing houses, museums, packaging firms, photography studios, marketing and public relations firms, desktop publishing outfits, digital pre-press houses, or printing companies. Art directors who oversee and produce on-screen products often work for film production houses, Web designers, multimedia developers, computer games developers, or television stations.

While companies of all sizes employ art directors, smaller organizations often combine the positions of graphic designer, illustrator, and art director. And although opportunities for art direction can be found all across the nation and abroad, many larger firms in such cities as Chicago, Los Angeles, and New York usually have more openings, as well as higher pay scales, than smaller companies.

STARTING OUT

Since an art director's job requires a great deal of experience, it is usually not considered an entry-level position. Typically, a person on a career track toward art director is hired as an assistant to an established director. Recent graduates wishing to enter advertising should have a portfolio of their work containing seven to 10 sample ads to demonstrate their understanding of both the business and the media in which they want to work.

Serving as an intern is a good way to get experience and develop skills. Graduates should also consider taking an entry-level job in a publisher's art department to gain initial experience. Either way, aspiring art directors must be willing to acquire their credentials by working on various projects. This may mean working in a variety of areas, such as advertising, design, editing, and marketing.

College publications offer students a chance to gain experience and develop portfolios. In addition, many students are able to do freelance work while still in school, allowing them to make important industry contacts and gain on-the-job experience at the same time.

ADVANCEMENT

While some may be content on reaching the position of art director, many art directors take on even more responsibility within their organizations, become television directors, start their own advertising agencies, create their own Web sites, develop original multimedia programs, or launch their own magazines.

Many people who get to the position of art director do not advance beyond the title but move on to work at more prestigious firms. Competition for positions at companies that have national reputations continues to be keen because of the sheer number of talented people interested. At smaller publications or local companies, competition may be less intense, since candidates are competing primarily against others in the local market.

EARNINGS

The job title of art director can mean many different things, depending on the company at which the director is employed. According to the U.S. Department of Labor, a beginning art director or an art director who worked at a small firm earned $37,920 or less per year in 2006, while experienced art directors working at larger companies earned more than $135,090. Mean annual earnings for art directors employed in the advertising industry (the largest employer of salaried art directors) were $82,680 in 2006. Median annual earnings for art directors working in all industries were $68,100. (Again, it is important to note that these positions are not entry level; beginning art directors have probably already accumulated several years of experience in the field for which they were paid far less.)

According to the American Institute of Graphic Arts/Aquent Salary Survey 2007, the median salary for art directors was $70,000. Art directors in the 25th percentile earned $55,000 annually, while those in the 75th percentile made $82,000 per year. Salaries varied by geographic region. For example, art directors in the Mid-Atlantic states had average salaries of $75,000 a year, while those in the Mountain region earned an average of $55,000.

Most companies employing art directors offer insurance benefits, a retirement plan, and other incentives and bonuses.

WORK ENVIRONMENT

Art directors usually work in studios or office buildings. While their work areas are ordinarily comfortable, well lit, and ventilated, they often handle glue, paint, ink, and other materials that pose safety hazards, and they should, therefore, exercise caution.

Art directors at art and design studios and publishing firms usually work a standard 40-hour week. Many, however, work overtime during busy periods to meet deadlines. Similarly, directors at film and video operations and at television studios work as many hours as required—usually many more than 40 per week—to finish projects according to predetermined schedules.

While art directors work independently reviewing artwork and reading copy, much of their time is spent collaborating with and supervising a team of employees, often consisting of copywriters, editors, photographers, graphic artists, and account executives.

OUTLOOK

The extent to which art director positions are in demand, like many other positions, depends on the economy in general; when times are tough, people and businesses spend less, and cutbacks are made. When the economy is healthy, employment prospects for art directors will be favorable. The U.S. Department of Labor predicts that employment for art directors will grow about as fast as the average for all occupations through 2016. One area that shows particularly good promise for growth is the retail industry, since more and more large retail establishments, especially catalog houses, will be employing in-house advertising art directors.

In addition, producers of all kinds of products continually need advertisers to reach their potential customers, and publishers always want some type of illustration to enhance their books and magazines. Creators of films and videos also need images to produce their programs, and people working with new media are increasingly looking for artists and directors to promote new and existing products and services, enhance their Web sites, develop new multimedia programs, and create multidimensional visuals. People who can quickly and creatively generate new concepts and ideas will be in high demand.

However, the supply of aspiring artists is expected to exceed the number of job openings. As a result, those wishing to enter the field will encounter keen competition for salaried, staff positions as well as for freelance work. And although the Internet is expected to provide many opportunities for artists and art directors, some firms are hiring employees without formal art or design training to operate computer-aided design systems and oversee work.

FOR MORE INFORMATION

The AAF is the professional advertising association that binds the mutual interests of corporate advertisers, agencies, media companies, suppliers, and academia. For more information, contact
American Advertising Federation (AAF)
1101 Vermont Avenue, NW, Suite 500
Washington, DC 20005-6306
Tel: 800-999-2231
Email: aaf@aaf.org
http://www.aaf.org

This management-oriented national trade organization represents the advertising agency business. For information, contact
American Association of Advertising Agencies
405 Lexington Avenue, 18th Floor
New York, NY 10174-1801
Tel: 212-682-2500
http://www.aaaa.org

For more information on design professionals, contact
American Institute of Graphic Arts
164 Fifth Avenue
New York, NY 10010-5901
Tel: 212-807-1990
http://www.aiga.org

The Art Directors Club is an international, nonprofit organization of directors in advertising, graphic design, interactive media, broadcast design, typography, packaging, environmental design, photography, illustration, and related disciplines. For information, contact
The Art Directors Club
106 West 29th Street
New York, NY 10001-5301
Tel: 212-643-1440
Email: info@adcny.org
http://www.adcglobal.org

For information on the graphic arts, contact
Graphic Artists Guild
32 Broadway, Suite 1114
New York, NY 10004-1612
Tel: 212-791-3400
http://www.gag.org

Buyers

OVERVIEW

There are two main types of *buyers*. *Wholesale buyers* purchase merchandise directly from manufacturers and resell it to retail firms, commercial establishments, and other institutions. *Retail buyers* purchase goods from wholesalers (and occasionally from manufacturers) for resale to the general public. In either case, buyers must understand their customers' needs and be able to purchase goods at an appropriate price and in sufficient quantity. Sometimes a buyer is referred to by the type of merchandise purchased—for example, jewelry buyer or toy buyer. There are approximately 5,000 buyers currently working in advertising and related industries in the United States.

HISTORY

The job of the buyer has been influenced by a variety of historical changes, including the growth of large retail stores in the 20th century. In the past, store owners typically performed almost all of the business activities, including the purchase of merchandise. Large stores, in contrast, had immensely more complicated operations, requiring large numbers of specialized workers, such as sales clerks, receiving and shipping clerks, advertising managers, personnel officers, and buyers. The introduction of mass production systems at factories required more complicated planning, ordering, and scheduling of purchases. A wider range of available merchandise also called for more astute selection and purchasing techniques.

THE JOB

Wholesale and retail buyers are part of a complex system of production, distribution, and merchandising. Both are concerned with recognizing and satisfying the huge variety of consumer needs and desires. Most specialize in acquiring one or two lines of merchandise.

Retail buyers work for retail stores. They generally can be divided into two types. The first, working directly under a merchandise manager, not only purchases goods but directly supervises salespeople. When a new product appears on the shelves, for example, buyers may work with salespeople to point out its distinctive features. This type of retail buyer thus takes responsibility for the product's marketing. The second type of retail buyer is concerned only with purchasing and has no supervisory responsibilities. These buyers cooperate with the sales staff to promote maximum sales.

All retail buyers must understand the basic merchandising policies of their stores. Purchases are affected by the size of the buyer's annual budget, the kind of merchandise needed in each buying season, and trends in the market. Success in buying is directly related to the profit or loss shown by particular departments. Buyers often work with *assistant buyers,* who spend much of their time maintaining sales and inventory records.

All buyers must be experts in the merchandise that they purchase. They order goods months ahead of their expected sale, and they must be able to predetermine marketability based on cost, style, and competitive items. Buyers must also be well acquainted with the best sources of supply for each product they purchase.

Depending on the location, size, and type of store, a retail buyer may deal directly with traveling salespeople (ordering from samples or catalogs), order by mail or by telephone directly from the manufacturer or wholesaler, or travel to key cities to visit merchandise showrooms and manufacturing establishments. Most use a combination of these approaches.

Buying trips to such cities as Chicago, New York, and San Francisco are an important part of the work for buyers at a larger store. For specialized products, such as glassware, china, liquors, and gloves, some buyers make yearly trips to major European production centers. Sometimes manufacturers of similar items organize trade shows to attract a number of buyers. Buying trips are difficult; a buyer may visit six to eight suppliers in a single day. The buyer must make decisions on the spot about the opportunity for the profitable sale of merchandise. The important element is not how much the buyer personally likes the merchandise but about customers' taste. Most buyers operate under an annual purchasing budget for the departments they represent.

Mergers between stores and expansion of individual department stores into chains of stores have created central buying positions. *Central buyers* order in unusually large quantities. As a result, they have the power to develop their own set of specifications for a particular item and ask manufacturers to bid on the right to provide it. Goods purchased by central buyers may be marketed under the manufacturer's label (as is normally done) or ordered with the store's label or a chain brand name.

To meet this competition, independent stores often work with *resident buyers*, who purchase merchandise for a large number of stores. By purchasing large quantities of the same product, resident buyers can obtain the same types of discounts enjoyed by large chain stores and then pass along the savings to their customers.

REQUIREMENTS
High School
A high school diploma generally is required to enter the field of buying. Useful high school courses include business, economics, English, and mathematics.

Postsecondary Training
A college degree may not be a requirement for becoming a buyer, but it is becoming increasingly important, especially for advancement. A majority of buyers have attended college, many majoring in business, economics, or engineering. Some colleges and universities also offer majors in purchasing or materials management. Regardless of the major, useful courses in preparation for a career in buying include accounting, advertising, commercial law, economics, finance, marketing, and various business classes, such as business communications, business organization and management, and computer applications in business.

Retailing experience is helpful to gain a sense of customer tastes and witness the supply and demand process. Additional training is available through trade associations, such as the Institute for Supply Management, which sponsors conferences, seminars, and workshops.

Certification or Licensing
Certification, although not required, is becoming increasingly important. Various levels of certification are available through the

American Purchasing Society and the Institute for Supply Management. To earn most certifications, you must have work experience, meet education requirements, and pass written and oral exams.

Other Requirements

If you are interested in becoming a buyer, you should be organized and have excellent decision-making skills. Predicting consumer tastes and keeping stores and wholesalers appropriately stocked requires resourcefulness, good judgment, and confidence. You should also have skills in marketing to identify and promote products that will sell. Finally, leadership skills are needed to supervise assistant buyers and deal with manufacturers' representatives and store executives.

EXPLORING

One way to explore the retailing field is through part-time or summer employment in a store. A good time to look for such work is during the Christmas holiday season. Door-to-door selling is another way to gain business retailing experience. Occasionally, experience in a retail store can be found through special high school programs.

EMPLOYERS

Approximately 5,000 buyers currently work in advertising and related industries in the United States. Buyers work for a wide variety of businesses, both wholesale and retail, as well as for government agencies. Employers range from small stores, where buying may be only one function of a manager's job, to multinational corporations, where a buyer may specialize in one type of item and buy in enormous quantity.

STARTING OUT

Most buyers find their first job by applying to the personnel office of a retail establishment or wholesaler. Because knowledge of retailing is important, buyers may be required to have work experience in a store.

Most buyers begin their careers as retail sales workers. The next step may be *head of stock*. The head of stock maintains stock inventory records and keeps the merchandise in a neat and well-organized fashion both to protect its value and to permit easy access. He or she usually supervises the work of several employees, and also works in an intermediate position between the salespeople on the floor and the buyer who provides the merchandise. The next step to becoming a buyer may be assistant buyer. For many department stores, promotion to full buyer requires this background.

Large department stores or chains operate executive training programs for college graduates who seek buying and other retail executive positions. A typical program consists of 16 successive weeks of work in a variety of departments. This on-the-job experience is supplemented by formal classroom work that most often is conducted by senior executives and training department personnel. Following this orientation, trainees are placed in junior management positions for an additional period of supervised experience and training.

ADVANCEMENT

Buyers are key employees of the stores or companies that employ them. One way they advance is through increased responsibility, such as more authority to make commitments for merchandise and more complicated buying assignments.

Buyers are sometimes promoted to *merchandise manager*, which requires them to supervise other buyers, help develop the store's merchandising policies, and coordinate buying and selling activities with related departments. Other buyers may become vice presidents in charge of merchandising or even store presidents. Because buyers learn much about retailing in their job, they are in a position to advance to top executive positions. Some buyers use their knowledge of retailing and the contacts they have developed with suppliers to set up their own businesses.

EARNINGS

How much a buyer earns depends on various factors, including the employer's sales volume. Mass merchandisers, such as discount or chain department stores, pay among the highest salaries.

The U.S. Department of Labor reports the median annual income for nonagricultural wholesale and retail buyers was $44,640 in 2006. The lowest paid 10 percent of these buyers made less than $26,270 yearly, and at the other end of the pay range, the highest paid 10 percent earned more than $83,080 annually.

Most buyers receive the usual benefits, such as vacation, sick leave, life and health insurance, and pension plans. Retail buyers may receive cash bonuses for their work as well as discounts on merchandise they purchase from their employer.

WORK ENVIRONMENT

Buyers work in a dynamic and sometimes stressful atmosphere. They must make important decisions on an hourly basis. The results of their work, both successes and failures, show up quickly on the profit and loss statement.

Buyers frequently work long or irregular hours. Evening and weekend hours are common, especially during the holiday season, when the retail field is at its busiest. Extra hours may be required to bring records up to date, for example, or to review stock and to become familiar with the store's overall marketing design for the coming season. Travel may also be a regular part of a buyer's job, possibly requiring several days away from home each month.

Although buyers must sometimes work under pressure, they usually work in pleasant, well-lit environments. They also benefit from having a diverse set of responsibilities.

OUTLOOK

Little or no employment growth is predicted for wholesale and retail buyers through 2016, according to the U.S. Department of Labor. Stagnant growth can be attributed to the large number of business mergers and acquisitions, which results in the blending of buying departments and the elimination of redundant jobs. In addition, the use of computers, which increases efficiency, and the trend of some large retail companies to centralize their operations will both contribute to fewer new jobs for buyers. Some job openings will result from the need to hire replacement workers for those who leave the field. On the other hand, companies in the service sector are beginning to realize the advantages of having professional buyers.

FOR MORE INFORMATION

For career information and job listings, contact
American Purchasing Society
PO Box 256
Aurora, IL 60506-0256
Tel: 630-859-0250
http://www.american-purchasing.com

For lists of colleges with purchasing programs and career information, contact
Institute for Supply Management
PO Box 22160
Tempe, AZ 85285-2160

Tel: 800-888-6276
http://www.ism.ws

For materials on educational programs in the retail industry, contact
National Retail Federation
325 7th Street, NW, Suite 1100
Washington, DC 20004-2818
Tel: 800-673-4692
http://www.nrf.com

Composers

QUICK FACTS

School Subjects
Music
Theater/dance

Personal Skills
Artistic
Communication/ideas

Work Environment
Primarily indoors
Primarily one location

Minimum Education Level
High school diploma

Salary Range
$15,210 to $39,750 to
$110,850+

Certification or Licensing
None available

Outlook
About as fast as the average

DOT
152

GOE
01.05.02

NOC
5132

O*NET-SOC
27-2041.02, 27-2041-03

OVERVIEW

Composers create much of the music heard every day on radio and television, on recordings and in advertising, in theaters and concert halls, and through any other medium of musical presentation. Composers write symphonies, concertos, and operas; scores for theater, television, and cinema; and music for musical theater, recording artists, and commercial advertising. They may combine elements of classical music with those of popular musical styles such as rock, jazz, reggae, folk, and others.

HISTORY

Classical (used in the widest sense) composition probably dates back to the late Middle Ages, when musical notation began to develop in Christian monasteries. In those times and for some centuries thereafter, the church was the main patron of musical composition. During the 14th century, or possibly earlier, the writing of music in score (that is, for several instruments or instruments and voices) began to take place. This was the beginning of a great change in the history of music. The craft of making musical instruments and the techniques of playing them were advancing also. By the beginning of the Baroque period, around 1600, these changes brought musical composition to a new stage of development, which was enhanced by patronage from non-religious sources. The nobility had taken an interest in sponsoring musical composition, and over the next two to three hundred years they came to supplant the church as the main patrons of compos-

54

ers. Under their patronage, composers had more room to experiment and develop new musical styles.

The "true" classical period in music began about the mid-18th century and lasted through the 19th century. Composers embellishing the sonata form now developed the symphony. Through the latter half of the 19th century, most composers of symphonies, concerti, chamber music, and other instrumental forms adhered to the strict formality of the classical tradition. In the 19th century, however, many composers broke from classical formalism, instilling greater emotionalism, subjectivity, and individualism in their work. The new musical style evolved into what became formally known as the Romantic movement in music. Romanticism did not replace classicism, but rather, it existed side by side with the older form.

Many of the composers of the early classical period labored for little more than recognition. Their monetary rewards were often meager. In the 19th century, however, as the stature of the composers grew, they were able to gain more control over their own work and the proceeds that it produced. Opera composers, in particular, were able to reap quite handsome profits.

Another abrupt break from tradition occurred at the beginning of the 20th century. At that time composers began to turn away from Romanticism and seek new and original styles and sounds. Audiences sometimes were repulsed by these new musical sounds, but eventually they were accepted and imitated by other composers. One of the most successful of the post-Romantic composers was Igor Stravinsky, whose landmark work *The Rite of Spring* was hailed by some to be the greatest work of the century.

Through the 20th century composers continued to write music in the styles of the past and to experiment with new styles. During this time composers began to create music for local and national radio and television advertising campaigns. While different in scope from longer performance pieces, music created for advertising campaigns is just as memorable, if not more so, in some cases. Soon products became synonymous with their advertising "jingles," such as Oscar Meyer's famous bologna campaign.

In the late 20th and early 21st centuries, music composition continued to evolve as composers moved even further from traditional forms and musical instruments. Experiments with electronically created music, in which an electronic instrument, such as a synthesizer, is used to compose and play music, created a new world of sounds that audiences came to love. Computers came to be used as compositional tools.

THE JOB

Composers express themselves in music much as writers express themselves with words and painters with line, shape, and color. Although influenced by what they hear, composers' compositions are original because they reflect their own interpretation and use of musical elements. All composers use the same basic musical elements, including harmony, melody, counterpoint, and rhythm, but each composer applies these elements in a unique way. Music schools teach all of the elements that go into composition, providing composers with the tools needed for their work, but how a composer uses these tools to create music is what sets an individual apart.

Composers may create compositions out of sheer inspiration, with or without a particular market in mind, or they may be commissioned to write a piece of music for a particular purpose (for example, for an advertising campaign, a film score, or an awards presentation). Composers who write music on their own must find someone to perform their music in the hopes that it will be well received and lead to further performances and possibly a recording. The more a composer's music is played and recorded, the greater the chances to sell future offerings and to receive commissions for new work. Commissions come from institutions (where the composer may or may not be a faculty member), societies and associations, and orchestral groups, or from film, television, and commercial projects. Almost every film has a score, the music playing throughout the film apart from any songs that may also be in the film.

A composer who wishes to make a living by writing music should know the musical marketplace as well as possible. Only a small percentage of music composers can make their living solely by writing music. To make a dent in the marketplace, one should be familiar with its major components: film, television, and advertising; performance; music publishing; copying; computerization; and recording.

Film, television, and advertising. There is a very large market for original compositions in feature and industrial films, television programs, radio and television advertising campaigns, and videos and DVDs. The industry is in constant need of original scores and thematic music. Working as a composer in this capacity requires a sound knowledge of both the project or product and the intended audience. *Jingle writers* are specialized composers who help businesses advertise their services or products via a short, memorable song, or jingle, used in television or radio commercials. At the start of a project, jingle writers meet with business owners or advertising agencies to establish guidelines for the jingle, such as the style of music, ideas or catch phrases, and the length of the jingle. Some advertising agencies may already have lyrics completed or partially written before contracting jingle writers for the melody. Other businesses may give jingle writers full creative control of the project. Once lyrics are set to music, jingle writers perform a demo for the client's approval. Most jingle writers are also musicians and often perform solo or alongside other musicians in the production of the jingle. The most successful jingle writers are creative, work well under pressure, and are talented musicians and arrangers. Most projects pay a flat fee for writing or arranging the jingle; however, a residual fee is given for those actually performing the piece.

Performance. Composers usually rely on one of two ways to have their music performed: they contact musical performers or producers who are most likely to be receptive to their style of composition, or they may write for a musical group in which they are performers.

Music publishing. Music publishers seek composers who are talented and whose work they feel it will be profitable to promote. They take a cut of the royalties, but they relieve composers of all of the business and legal details of their profession. Composers today have rather commonly turned to self-publishing.

Copying. A musical composition written for several pieces or voices requires copying into various parts. Composers may do this work themselves, but it is an exacting task for which professional copiers may be employed. Many composers themselves take on copying work as a sideline.

Computerization. Computers have become an increasingly important tool for composing and copying. Some composers have set up incredibly sophisticated computerized studios in which they compose, score, and play an orchestrated piece by computer. They can also do the copying and produce a recording. Perhaps the most significant enhancement to the home studio is the Musical Instrument Digital Interface, which transposes the composer's work into computer language and then converts it into notation.

Recording. Knowing the recording industry is an important aspect in advancing a composer's career. An unrecognized composer will find it difficult to catch on with a commercial recording company, but it is not uncommon for a composer to make his own recording and handle the distribution and promotion as well.

REQUIREMENTS

High School

There is no specific course of training that leads one to become a composer. Musically inclined students should continue their private studies and take advantage of everything musical their high school offers. Specially gifted students usually find their way to schools or academies that specialize in music or the arts. These students may begin learning composition in this special environment, and some might begin to create original compositions.

Postsecondary Training

After high school, musical students can continue their education in any of numerous colleges and universities or special music schools or conservatories that offer bachelor's and higher degrees. The composer's course of study includes courses on music history, music criticism, music theory, harmony, counterpoint, rhythm, melody, and ear training. In most major music schools courses in composition are offered along with orchestration and arranging. Courses are also taught covering voice and the major musical instruments, including keyboard, guitar, and, more recently, synthesizer. Most schools now cover computer techniques as applied to music as well. It may also be helpful to learn at least one foreign language; German, French, and Italian are good choices.

If working as a composer in the film, television, radio, or advertising industries appeals to you, consider combining your music studies with a major in communications or business to help diversify your knowledge of an industry.

Other Requirements

Prospective composers are advised to become proficient on at least one instrument.

Study in a musical institution is not a requirement for a composer, nor is it any guarantee of success. Some say that composing cannot be taught, that the combination of skills, talent, and inspiration required to create music is a highly individual occurrence. Authorities have argued on both sides of this issue without resolution. It does appear that genetics plays a strong part in musical ability; musical people often come from musical families. There are many contradictions of this, however, and some authorities cite the musical environment as being highly influential. The great composers were extraordinarily gifted, and it is very possible that achieving even moderate success in music requires special talent. Nevertheless, there will be little success without hard work and dedication.

Composers employed in advertising and related industries must
have a flair for turning ideas and concepts into catchy and appealing
music and words that will convince customers to purchase a company's products or services. They must be able to create jingles under
tight deadlines and be comfortable receiving constructive criticism
of their work. Composers should also have musical talent and excellent writing skills.

EXPLORING

Musical programs offered by local schools, YMCAs, and community centers offer good beginning opportunities. It is especially helpful to learn to play a musical instrument, such as the piano, violin,
or cello. Attending concerts and recitals and reading about music
and musicians and their careers will also provide good background
and experience. Young musicians should form or join musical groups
and attempt to write music for the groups to perform. Many books
and DVDs are available that provide good reference information on
careers in composing.

EMPLOYERS

Most composers are self-employed. They complete their work in
their own studios and then try to sell their pieces to music publishers,
film and television production companies, or recording companies.
Once their work becomes well known, clients, such as film and television producers, dance companies, or musical theater producers,
may commission original pieces from composers. In this case, the
client provides a story line, time period, mood, and other specifications the composer must honor in the creation of a musical score.

There might be a few "house" composer jobs in advertising agencies or studios that make commercials, or at film, television, and
video production studios. Schools often underwrite a composer in
residence, and many composers work as professors in college and
university music departments while continuing to compose. For the
most part, however, composers are on their own to create and promote their work.

STARTING OUT

In school, young composers should try to have their work performed either at school concerts or by local school or community
ensembles. This will also most likely involve the composers in copying and scoring their work and possibly even directing. Student

film projects can provide an opportunity for experience at film composing and scoring. Working in school or local musical theater companies can also provide valuable experience. Personal connections made in these projects may be very helpful in the professional world that lies ahead. Developing a portfolio of work will be useful as the composer enters a professional career.

Producers of public service announcements, or PSAs, for radio and television are frequently on the lookout for pro bono (volunteer) work that can provide opportunities for young, willing composers. Such opportunities may be listed in trade magazines, such as *Variety* (available in print or online at http://www.variety.com) and *Show Business* (in print or online at http://showbusinessweekly.com).

Joining the American Federation of Musicians and other musical societies and associations is another good move for aspiring composers. Among the associations that can be contacted are Meet the Composer, Broadcast Music, Inc., and the American Society of Composers, Authors, and Publishers (ASCAP), all located in New York City. These associations and the trade papers are also valuable sources for leads on grants and awards for which composers can apply.

Young composers, songwriters, and jingle writers can also work their way into the commercial advertising business by doing some research and taking entry-level jobs with agencies that handle musical commercials.

ADVANCEMENT

Moving ahead in the music world is done strictly on an individual basis. There is no hierarchical structure to climb, although in record companies a person with music writing talent might move into a producing or A&R (Artists & Repertoire) job and be able to exercise compositional skills in those capacities. Advancement is based on talent, determination, and, probably, luck. Some composers become well known for their work with film scores, such as John Williams of *Star Wars* fame.

Advancement for composers often takes place on a highly personal level. They may progress through their careers to writing music of greater complexity and in more challenging structures. They may develop a unique style and even create new forms and traditions of music. One day, their name might be added to the list of great composers.

Composers employed in the advertising industry can advance by working for larger agencies or by achieving higher salaries and name recognition as a result of writing award-winning jingles.

EARNINGS

A few composers make huge annual incomes, while many make little or nothing. Some earn a very large income in one or two years and none in succeeding years. While many composers receive royalties on repeat performances of their work, most depend on commissions to support themselves. Commissions vary widely according to the type of work and the industry for which the work will be performed. The U.S. Department of Labor reports that the median yearly income for music directors and composers holding salaried positions was $39,750 in 2006. Even for those in salaried positions, however, earnings range widely. The lowest paid 10 percent of this group made less than $15,210 in 2006, while the highest paid 10 percent earned more than $110,850. Many composers, however, do not hold full-time salaried positions and are only paid in royalties for their compositions that sell. According to ASCAP, the royalty rate for 2005 was $.085 per song per album sold. The $.085 is divided between the composer and the publisher, based on their agreement. If the album sold 25,000 copies in 2005, the royalties the composer and publisher received would be $2,125. Naturally, if this song is the only one the composer has that brings in income during this time, his or her annual earnings are extremely low (keep in mind that the composer receives only a percentage of the $2,125).

Many composers must hold a second job to make ends meet financially. In some cases these second jobs, such as teaching, will provide health insurance and paid vacation time. Composers who work independently, however, need to provide insurance and other benefits for themselves.

WORK ENVIRONMENT

The physical conditions of a composer's workplace can vary according to personal taste and affordability. Some work in expensive, state-of-the-art home studios, others in a bare room with an electric keyboard or a guitar. An aspiring composer may work in a cramped and cluttered room in a New York City tenement or in a Hollywood ranch home.

For the serious composer, the work is likely to be personally rewarding but financially unrewarding. For the commercial writer, some degree of financial reward is more likely, but competition is fierce, and the big prize goes only to the rarest of individuals. Getting started requires great dedication and sacrifice. Even those protected by academia must give up most of their spare time to compose, often sitting down the piano when exhausted from a full day of teaching. There are many frustrations along the way. The career composer must learn to live with rejection and have the verve and determination to keep coming back time and again. Under these circumstances, composers can only succeed by having complete faith in their own work.

OUTLOOK

The U.S. Department of Labor (USDL), which classifies composers in the category of musicians, singers, and related workers, predicts employment in this field to grow about as fast as the average for all occupations through 2016. Although no reliable statistics exist on the number of people who make their living solely from composing, the general consensus is that very few people can sustain themselves through composing alone. The field is extremely competitive and crowded with highly talented people trying to have their music published and played. Only a limited number of commissions, grants, and awards are available at any time, and the availability of these is often subjected to changes in the economy. On the other hand, many films continue to be made each year, particularly as cable television companies produce more and more original programs. However, the chances of new composers supporting themselves by their music alone will likely always remain small.

The USDL predicts that employment in the advertising and public relations industries will grow faster than the average for all industries. Composers and jingle writers employed in these industries should also have good opportunities. There will always be a need for creative people to help companies craft jingles and commercials to help sell products and services—especially in today's highly competitive consumer marketplace.

FOR MORE INFORMATION

For professional and artistic development resources, contact
American Composers Forum
332 Minnesota Street, Suite East 145
St. Paul, MN 55101-1300
Tel: 651-228-1407
http://www.composersforum.org

For music news, news on legislation affecting musicians, and the magazine International Musician, *contact*

American Federation of Musicians of the United States and Canada
1501 Broadway, Suite 600
New York, NY 10036-5505
Tel: 212-869-1330
http://www.afm.org

For industry news, information on workshops and awards, and practical information about the business of music, contact

American Society of Composers, Authors, and Publishers
One Lincoln Plaza
New York, NY 10023-7129
Tel: 800-95-ASCAP
http://www.ascap.com

This organization represents songwriters, composers, and music publishers. Its Web site has useful information on the industry.

Broadcast Music, Inc.
320 West 57th Street
New York, NY 10019-3790
Tel: 212-586-2000
http://www.bmi.com

The Meet the Composer Web site has information on awards and residencies as well as interviews with composers active in the field today.

Meet the Composer
75 Ninth Avenue, 3R Suite C
New York, NY 10011-7006
Tel: 212-645-6949
http://www.meetthecomposer.org

For information on student membership and commission competitions, contact

Society of Composers
Box 450
New York, NY 10113-0450
http://www.societyofcomposers.org

For information on work in film, television, and multimedia, contact
> Society of Composers & Lyricists
> 400 South Beverly Drive, Suite 214
> Beverly Hills CA 90212-4414
> Tel: 310-281-2812
> http://www.thescl.com/site/scl

At select cities, the SGA offers song critiques and other workshops. Visit its Web site for further information on such events.
> **Songwriters Guild of America (SGA)**
> 1560 Broadway, Suite 408
> New York, NY 10036-1518
> Tel: 212-768-7902
> http://www.songwriters.org

INTERVIEW

Joyce Messina is co-owner (with her husband, Frank) of JoJo's Jingles in Oregon, a company that creates words and music for the advertising industry. (Visit http://www.jojosjingles.com to hear her work.) Joyce discussed her career with the editors of Careers in Focus: Advertising and Marketing.

Q. Why did you decide to become a jingle writer?

A. I became a jingle writer because my husband asked me to write the lyrics to music he was writing for a Broadway show. I was "bitten" by the lyric-writing bug and decided that jingle writing might be something I would enjoy. My love of music and poetry has made this a perfect match. A jingle is poetry in motion; sometimes humorous, sometimes serious, but always rhythmic.

Q. What are the main qualities of a good jingle?

A. A good jingle has a clear, understandable message with the facts that the advertiser wishes to communicate, a memorable phrase, and a good melody.

Q. What are the most important qualities for jingle writers?

A. Jingle writers should be musical and enjoy the excitement of creative thoughts. Seek out companies that you think could best use your services, online or door-to-door. Listen to prospective customers so that your jingle reflects what they are trying to sell.

Q. What advice would you give to high school students who are interested in this career?

A. It is important for a jingle writer to be a musician or have a musician who will work with you, as needed. In high school, you could offer to write jingles for any of the service clubs, the school newspaper, or local business establishments. If you have a music studio in your town, try to intern there or at an advertising agency. A good knowledge of English and writing is very important. Classes in poetry or fiction writing are also good prerequisites. Participating in band and drama is another factor that would increase your knowledge base and add to your creativity. Classes in marketing and small business administration are a must for your own business. Talk with others in the jingle business.

Copywriters

QUICK FACTS

School Subjects
English
Journalism

Personal Skills
Communication/ideas
Helping/teaching

Work Environment
Primarily indoors
Primarily one location

Minimum Education Level
Bachelor's degree

Salary Range
$25,430 to $60,250 to
$97,700+

Certification or Licensing
None available

Outlook
Faster than the average

DOT
131

GOE
01.02.01

NOC
5121

O*NET-SOC
27-3043.00

OVERVIEW

Copywriters express, promote, and interpret ideas and facts in written form for books, magazines, trade journals, newspapers, technical studies and reports, company newsletters, radio and television broadcasts, and advertisements.

Most copywriters are employed in the advertising industry. Their main goal is to persuade the general public to choose or favor certain goods, services, and personalities.

HISTORY

In its earliest days, advertising allowed merchants to go from street to shop, adopting symbols and later written signs to show the goods and services they offered. With the invention of paper and advances in education that enabled more and more people to read, tack-up signs became common. It wasn't until printing was introduced in the 15th century, however, that advertising was truly revolutionized. Merchants began printing and distributing handbills by the hundreds. Advertisements in newspapers became a familiar sight by the 17th century. By the end of the 1800s, magazines were carrying ads of all kinds.

In 1865, a new system was introduced to newspapers: the selling of space specifically for advertisers. Over time ads could be seen on huge outdoor billboards, between your favorite television shows, and on radio broadcasts. Today, the Internet has revolutionized the advertising industry, allowing advertisers not only to reach a new audience, but to interact with them as well.

THE JOB

Advertisements were once written and arranged by the individual or company selling a good or service. Today, most national and much local advertising, is prepared by advertising agencies. Modern firms split up the different tasks of advertising among workers specifically trained to handle the writing, design, and overall appearance of ads. Copywriters and their assistants write the words of advertisements, including the written text in print ads and the spoken words in radio and television ads, which are also called spots.

Copywriters may have to come up with their own idea and words for an ad, but generally the client's account manger and head designer generate the idea. Once the idea behind the ad is presented, copywriters begin gathering as much information as possible about the client through library research, interviews, the Internet, observation, and other methods. They study advertising trends and review surveys of consumer preferences. They keep extensive notes from which they will draw material for the ad. Once their research has been organized, copywriters begin working on the written components of the ad. They may have a standard theme or "pitch" to work with that has been developed in previous ads. One such example, using what is called a tagline, is seen in the popular milk campaigns promoting its health benefits and other advantages—beauty, athleticism, and intelligence: "Milk: It does a body good."

The process of developing copy is exciting, although it can also involve detailed and solitary work. After researching one idea, a writer might discover that a different perspective or related topic would be more effective, entertaining, or marketable.

When working on assignment, copywriters submit their ad drafts to their editor or the advertising account executive for approval. Writers will probably work through several drafts, writing and rewriting sections of the material as they proceed, searching for just the right way to promote the product, service, or other client need.

Copywriters, like other corporate writers, may also write articles, bulletins, news releases, sales letters, speeches, and other related informative and promotional material. Many copywriters are employed in advertising agencies. They also may work for marketing firms, public relations firms, or in communications departments of large companies.

Copywriters can be employed either as in-house staff or as free-lancers. Pay varies according to experience and the position, but freelancers must provide their own office space and equipment such as computers and fax machines. Freelancers also are responsible for keeping tax records, sending out invoices, negotiating contracts, and providing their own health insurance.

REQUIREMENTS

High School

While in high school, build a broad educational foundation by taking courses in business, computer science, English, foreign languages, literature, and typing. You should be confident in your typing abilities and comfortable with computer programs, as copywriters use computers every day for ad writing, researching, and development.

Postsecondary Training

Competition for writing jobs almost always demands the background of a college education. Many employers prefer that you have a broad liberal arts background or a major in English, history, literature, philosophy, or one of the social sciences. Other employers desire communications or journalism training in college. A number of schools offer courses in copywriting and other business writing.

In addition to formal course work, most employers look for practical writing experience. If you have served on high school or college newspapers, yearbooks, or literary magazines, you will make a better candidate, as well as if you have worked for small community newspapers or radio stations, even in an unpaid position. Many advertising agencies and public relations firms offer summer internship programs that can provide valuable writing experience. Interns do many simple tasks, such as running errands and answering phones, but some may be asked to perform research and even assist with the ad writing.

Other Requirements

To be a copywriter, you should be creative and able to express ideas clearly, have a broad general knowledge, be a skilled researcher, and be computer literate. Other assets include curiosity, persistence, initiative, resourcefulness, and an accurate memory. At some ad agencies and other employers, the environment is hectic and client deadlines are short. For these copywriters, the ability to concentrate and produce under pressure is essential.

Other Opportunities in Advertising and Marketing

The advertising and marketing industries offer a variety of career paths to people from all educational backgrounds. Here are just a few of the additional options not covered in detail in this book:

- Accountants and auditors
- Bookkeeping, accounting, and auditing clerks
- Computer and Internet security specialists
- Computer programmers
- Computer software engineers
- Customer service representatives
- Data entry and information processing workers
- Editors
- Intellectual property lawyers
- Mail clerks and mail machine operators
- Multimedia artists and animators
- Network and computer systems administrators
- Office clerks
- Printers
- Producers
- Receptionists
- Security workers
- Web developers
- Webmasters

EXPLORING

As a high school or college student, you can test your interest and aptitude in the field of writing by serving as a reporter or writer on school newspapers, yearbooks, and literary magazines. Various writing courses and workshops will offer you the opportunity to sharpen your writing skills.

Small community newspapers and local radio stations often welcome contributions from outside sources, although they may not have the resources to pay for them. Jobs in bookstores, magazine shops, and even newsstands will offer you a chance to become familiar with various publications.

You can also obtain information on writing as a career by visiting local newspapers, publishers, or radio and television stations and interviewing some of the writers who work there. Career conferences and other guidance programs frequently include speakers on the entire field of communications from local or national organizations.

EMPLOYERS

Approximately 19,200 advertising firms are located nationwide, employing more than 300,000 workers. Copywriters and editors hold approximately 10,000 jobs in the industry.

STARTING OUT

Most copywriters start out in entry-level positions, working as office assistants or copywriting assistants. These jobs may be listed with college career services offices or in the want ads of local papers and on the Internet. You can also try applying directly to the hiring departments of the advertising agencies or other large companies that have public relations departments. Graduates who previously served internships with these companies often have the advantage of knowing someone who can give them a personal recommendation.

Employers will often ask to see samples of published writing. These samples should be assembled in an organized portfolio or scrapbook. Bylined or signed articles are more credible (and, as a result, more useful) than stories whose source is not identified.

Beginning positions as a copywriting assistant usually involve library research, preparation of rough ad drafts, and other related writing tasks. These are generally carried on under the supervision of a senior copywriter.

ADVANCEMENT

Advancement may be more rapid in small advertising agencies or companies, where beginners learn by doing a little bit of everything and may be given writing tasks immediately. In large firms, duties are usually more compartmentalized. Assistants in entry-level positions are assigned such tasks as research, fact checking, and copywriting, but it generally takes much longer to advance to full-scale copywriting duties.

Promotion as a copywriter usually takes the form of obtaining more projects for larger and more influential clients. For example, being assigned to work on spots for a large corporation would be viewed as an impressive achievement. Others advance by moving to a larger or more prestigious firm or starting their own business.

Freelance or self-employed writers earn advancement in the form of larger fees as they gain exposure and establish their reputations.

EARNINGS

According to the U.S. Department of Labor (USDL), median annual salaries for writers in advertising and related services were $60,250 in 2006. In 2006, median annual earnings for all salaried writers (including copywriters) were $48,640 a year, according to the USDL. The lowest paid 10 percent earned less than $25,430, while the highest paid 10 percent earned $97,700 or more.

In addition to their salaries, many writers earn income from freelance work. Part-time freelancers may earn from $5,000 to $15,000 a year. Freelance earnings vary widely. Full-time established freelance writers may earn more than $75,000 a year.

WORK ENVIRONMENT

Working conditions vary for copywriters, depending on the size of their employer and whether they frequently work under tight deadlines. Though their workweek usually runs 35 to 40 hours, many copywriters work overtime, working nights and weekends to meet client deadlines.

Although copywriters do some of their work independently, they often must cooperate with artists, photographers, editors, and other advertising people who may have widely differing ideas of how the materials should be prepared and presented.

Physical surroundings range from comfortable private offices to noisy, crowded offices filled with other workers typing and talking on the telephone. Some copywriters must confine their research to the library or telephone interviews, but others may travel to other cities or countries or to client worksites.

The work is arduous, but most copywriters are seldom bored. The most difficult element is the continual pressure of deadlines. People who are the most content as copywriters enjoy and work well with deadline pressure.

OUTLOOK

The outlook for the advertising industry as a whole looks promising, according to the USDL. Overall employment is projected to grow 14 percent through 2016 (or faster than the average of 11 percent predicted for all industries). Smaller agencies and home-based businesses are on the rise; however, the mega-agencies—multinational agencies created from mergers and acquisitions—still dominate the industry. Of the 48,000 advertising and public relations agencies in the United States, most of the large firms are located in Chicago, Los Angeles, and New York, and offer higher pay scales than smaller agencies. Employment for writers and authors in the advertising industry is projected to grow by 8 percent through 2016 (or about as fast as the average for all occupations).

Another important trend that will affect the employment of copywriters is specialization. Many agencies are increasing their focus on niche markets, and they will continue to specialize. Expected high-growth areas include foreign-language programming, advertising aimed at specific ethnic groups, advertising targeted at the over-50 market, special events advertising and marketing, and direct marketing campaigns for retailers and technological companies. Copywriters who can offer skills such as the ability to speak and write in a foreign language will be in demand.

In addition, the explosion of online advertising has created a wealth of jobs. The number of Internet users as of January 2007 was 1.094 billion, and companies are responding by placing advertising on the Web and creating Web sites that allow customers the ease and convenience of online shopping. From flowers to antiques, clothing to furniture, virtually everything can be purchased online. All of these goods and services require copywriters to write ads that will promote and sell. Individuals with extensive computer skills will be at an advantage as a result.

People entering this field should realize that the competition for jobs is extremely keen. The appeal of writing and advertising jobs will continue to grow, as many young graduates find the industry glamorous and exciting.

FOR MORE INFORMATION

For profiles of advertising workers and career information, contact
Advertising Educational Foundation
220 East 42nd Street, Suite 3300
New York, NY 10017-5806

Tel: 212-986-8060
http://www.aef.com

Visit this organization's Web site to learn more about internships, scholarships, and awards.
American Advertising Federation
1101 Vermont Avenue, NW, Suite 500
Washington, DC 20005-6306
Tel: 800-999-2231
Email: aaf@aaf.org
http://www.aaf.org

For industry information, contact
American Association of Advertising Agencies
405 Lexington Avenue, 18th Floor
New York, NY 10174-1801
Tel: 212-682-2500
http://www.aaaa.org

Demographers

QUICK FACTS

School Subjects
Computer science
Mathematics
Sociology

Personal Skills
Communication/ideas
Technical/scientific

Work Environment
Primarily indoors
One location with some
   travel

Minimum Education Level
Bachelor's degree

Salary Range
$38,230 to $64,920 to
$103,390+

Certification or Licensing
None available

Outlook
About as fast as the average

DOT
054

GOE
02.04.02, 02.06.02

NOC
2161

O*NET-SOC
15-2041.00, 19-3099.00

OVERVIEW

Demographers are population specialists who collect and analyze vital statistics related to human population changes, such as births, marriages, and deaths. They plan and conduct research surveys to study population trends and assess the effects of population movements. Demographers work for government organizations as well as at private companies across the country.

HISTORY

Population studies of one kind or another have always been of interest for various reasons. As early as the mid-1600s, for example, the English were the first to systematically record and register all births and deaths. Over the years, recording techniques were refined and expanded to conduct more sophisticated population surveys so that governments could collect information, such as number of people and extent of property holdings, to measure wealth and levy taxes.

In recent years, census taking has become much more comprehensive, and the scientific methods of collecting and interpreting demographic information have also improved extensively. Demographers now have a leading role in developing detailed population studies that are designed to reveal the essential characteristics of a society, such as the availability of health care or average income levels.

THE JOB

Demography is a social science that organizes population facts into a statistical analysis. A demographer works to establish ways in which numbers may be organized to produce new and useful information. For example, demographers may study data collected on the growth of the Hispanic population in a certain region, develop graphs and charts to detail the changes in this population, and then forecast the probability that this growth may continue. This information might be used by a company that is seeking to market products to Hispanic people.

Many demographers work on the basis of a "sampling" technique in which the characteristics of the whole population are judged by taking a sample of a part of it. For example, demographers may collect data on the educational level of residents living in various locations throughout a community. They can use this information to make a projection of the average educational level of the community as a whole. In this way, demographers conduct research and forecast trends on various social and economic patterns throughout an area. A marketing firm employed by a community college might use this data when preparing a marketing campaign that seeks to educate potential adult students about academic programs at the school. If the data reveals that a high percentage of adults in the community already have an associate's degree, then the firm might rethink its plan to target this demographic group. If research reveals a high number of adults with only a high school diploma, the firm might move forward and develop a marketing campaign to reach these potential students.

Demographers not only conduct their own surveys but often work with statistics gathered from government sources, private surveys, and public opinion polls. They may compare different statistical information, such as an area's average income level and its population, and use it to forecast the community's future educational and medical needs. They may also use this information to help advertisers and marketers reach target audiences.

Computers have radically changed the role of the demographer. Now, much greater amounts of data can be collected and analyzed. In the Bureau of Census, for example, demographers work with material that has been compiled from the nationwide census conducted every 10 years. Millions of pieces of demographic information, such as age, gender, occupation, educational level, and country of origin, are collected from people around the country. A demographer may take this statistical information, analyze it, and then use it to forecast population growth or economic trends.

Demographers investigate and analyze a variety of social science questions for the government, such as rates of illness, availability of health and police services, and other issues that define a community.

Private companies may use the information to make marketing, advertising, or public relations decisions, such as where to open a new store and how best to reach possible customers.

Demographers may work on long-range planning. Population trends are especially important in such areas as educational and economic planning, and a demographer's analysis is often used to help set policy on health care issues and a host of other social concerns. Local, state, and national government agencies use the demographer's statistical forecasts in an attempt to accurately provide transportation, education, and other services.

Demographers may teach demographic research techniques to students. They also work as consultants to private businesses. Much of their time is spent doing library research, analyzing demographic information of various population groups.

An *applied statistician,* a specialized type of demographer, uses accepted theories and known statistical formulas to collect and analyze data in a specific area. They may forecast population growth or economic conditions, predict and evaluate the result of an advertising or marketing program, or help companies develop various products.

REQUIREMENTS

High School
Since you will need at least a bachelor's degree to find work as a demographer, you should take college preparatory courses, such as English, mathematics (algebra and geometry), and social studies while in high school. In addition, take any statistics classes that your school offers. Training in computer science is also advantageous, as computers are used extensively for research and statistical analysis.

Postsecondary Training
College course work should include classes in computer applications, public health, public policy, social research methods, and statistics. Keep in mind that while you can get some starting jobs in the field with a bachelor's degree, most social scientists go on to attain advanced degrees. Many demographers get a doctorate in demography, sociology, or statistics. More than 200 colleges and universities offer degree programs in biostatistics, mathematics, and statistics.

Other Requirements
To work as a demographer, you should enjoy using logic to solve problems and have an aptitude for mathematics. You should also

enjoy detailed work and must like to study and learn. Research experience is helpful. Other helpful qualities include intellectual curiosity and creativity, good written and oral communication skills, objectivity, and systematic work habits.

EXPLORING

A part-time or summer job at a company with a statistical research department is a good way of gaining insight into the career of demographer. Discussions with professional demographers are another way of learning about the rewards and responsibilities in this field. While in high school, ask your mathematics teachers to give you some simple statistical problems related to population changes to practice the kinds of statistical techniques that demographers use. Exploring statistical surveys and information from The Gallup Organization on the Internet (http://www.gallup.com) is another way to learn about this career. Additionally, undertaking your own demographic survey of an organization or group, such as your school or after-school club, is a project worth considering.

EMPLOYERS

Federal agencies such as the Census Bureau and the Bureau of Labor Statistics employ a large number of demographers, as do local and state government agencies. Private industry (including large advertising and marketing firms) also may use the services of demographers, as well as universities, colleges, and foundations. Some demographers work as independent consultants rather than full-time employees for any one organization.

STARTING OUT

The usual method of entering the profession is through completion of an undergraduate or graduate degree in sociology or public health with an emphasis in demographic methods. According to Cary Davis, former vice president of the Population Reference Bureau in Washington, D.C., however, most entry-level positions require a graduate degree. "In fact," says Davis, "no one on my staff knew of any demographer who has less than a master's degree. Focus on an area that interests you, such as births and deaths or public health."

Qualified applicants can apply directly to private research firms or other companies that do population studies. University career services offices can help identify such organizations. Government jobs are listed with the Office of Personnel Management (http://www.usajobs.gov).

ADVANCEMENT

According to Davis, demographers who narrow their focus and become specialized in an area of interest are most likely to advance. Those with the highest degree of education are also most favored to be promoted.

EARNINGS

Earnings vary widely according to education, training, and place of employment. Social scientists earned a median annual salary of approximately $64,920 in 2006, according to the U.S. Department of Labor. Salaries ranged from less than $38,230 to more than $103,390. In 2006, statisticians (a career that often includes demographers) had median annual earnings of $65,720.

Vacation days and other benefits, such as sick leave, group insurance, and a retirement plan, are typically offered to demographers working full time for any large organization.

WORK ENVIRONMENT

Most demographers work in offices or classrooms during a regular 40-hour week. Depending on the project and deadlines, however, overtime may be required. Those engaged in research may work with other demographers assembling related information. Most of the work revolves around analyzing population data or interpreting computer information. A demographer is also usually responsible for writing a report detailing the findings. Some travel may be required, such as to attend a conference or complete limited field research.

OUTLOOK

According to the U.S. Department of Labor, careers in the social sciences are expected to grow about as fast as the average for all occupations through 2016. Those with the most training and greatest amount of education, preferably a Ph.D., should find the best job prospects. Employment opportunities should be greatest in and around large metropolitan areas, where many colleges, universities, research facilities, advertising and marketing firms, corporations, and federal agencies are located. Individuals with statistical training will have an advantage.

FOR MORE INFORMATION

For career publications, lists of accredited schools, and job information, contact
American Sociological Association
1307 New York Avenue, NW, Suite 700
Washington, DC 20005-4712
Tel: 202-383-9005
http://www.asanet.org

This organization includes demographers, sociologists, economists, public health professionals, and other individuals interested in research and education in the population field. For information on job opportunities, publications, and annual conferences and workshops, contact
Population Association of America
8630 Fenton Street, Suite 722
Silver Spring, MD 20910-3812
Tel: 301-565-6710
http://www.popassoc.org

For publications, special reports, and global population information, contact
Population Reference Bureau
1875 Connecticut Avenue, NW, Suite 520
Washington, DC 20009-5728
Tel: 800-877-9881
Email: popref@prb.org
http://www.prb.org

For population statistics, as well as information on regional offices, jobs, and a calendar of events, contact
U.S. Census Bureau
4700 Silver Hill Road
Washington, DC 20233-0001
Tel: 800-923-8282
http://www.census.gov

Graphic Designers

QUICK FACTS

School Subjects
Art
Computer science

Personal Skills
Artistic
Communication/ideas

Work Environment
Primarily indoors
Primarily one location

Minimum Education Level
Some postsecondary training

Salary Range
$20,000 to $45,590 to
$100,000+

Certification or Licensing
None available

Outlook
Much faster than the average

DOT
141

GOE
01.04.02

NOC
5241

O*NET-SOC
27-1024.00

OVERVIEW

Graphic designers are practical artists whose creations are intended to express ideas, convey information, or draw attention to a product. They design a wide variety of materials including advertisements, marketing pieces, displays, packaging, signs, computer graphics and games, book and magazine covers and interiors, animated characters, and company logos to fit the needs and preferences of their various clients. There are approximately 23,000 graphic designers employed in advertising and related industries in the United States.

HISTORY

The challenge of combining beauty, function, and technology in whatever form has preoccupied artisans throughout history. Graphic design work has been used to create products and promote commerce for as long as people have used symbols, pictures, and typography to communicate ideas.

Graphic design grew alongside the development of print media (newspapers, magazines, catalogs, and advertising). Typically, the graphic designer would sketch several rough drafts of the layout of pictures and words. After one of the drafts was approved, the designer would complete a final layout including detailed type and artwork specifications. The words were sent to a typesetter and the artwork assigned to an illustrator. When the final pieces were returned, the designer or a keyline and paste-up artist would adhere them with rubber cement or wax to an illustration board. Different colored items were placed on acetate overlays. This camera-ready art was now ready to be sent to a printer for photographing and reproduction.

Computer technology has revolutionized the way many graphic designers do their work. Today it is possible to be a successful graphic designer even if you can't draw more than simple stick figures. Graphic designers are now able to draw, color, and revise the many different images they work with using computers. They can choose typefaces, size type, and place images without having to manually align them on the page using a T square and triangle. Computer graphics enable graphic designers to work more quickly, since details like size, shape, and color are easy to change.

Graphics design programs are continually revised and improved, moving more and more design work from the artist's table to the computer mousepad and graphics tablet. As computer technology continues to advance in the areas of graphics and multimedia, more designers will have to know how to work with virtual reality applications.

THE JOB

Graphic designers are not primarily fine artists, although they may be highly skilled at drawing or painting. Most designs commissioned to graphic designers involve both artwork and copy (words). Thus, the designer must not only be familiar with the wide range of art media (photography, drawing, painting, collage, etc.) and styles, but he or she must also be familiar with a wide range of typefaces and know how to manipulate them for the right effect. Because design tends to change in a similar way to fashion, designers must keep up to date with the latest trends. At the same time, they must be well grounded in more traditional, classic designs.

Graphic designers can work as *in-house designers* for a particular company, as *staff designers* for a graphic design firm, or as *freelance designers* working for themselves. Some designers specialize in designing advertising materials or packaging. Others focus on corporate identity materials such as company stationery and logos. Some work mainly for publishers, designing book and magazine covers and page layouts. Some work in the area of computer graphics, creating still or animated graphics for computer software, videos, or motion pictures. A highly specialized type of graphic designer, the *environmental graphic designer,* designs large outdoor signs. Depending on the project's requirements, some graphic designers work exclusively on the computer, while others may use both the computer and drawings or paintings created by hand.

Whatever the specialty and whatever their medium, all graphic designers take a similar approach to a project, whether it is for an entirely new design or for a variation on an existing one. Graphic designers begin by determining the needs and preferences of clients and potential users, buyers, or viewers.

For example, if a graphic designer is working on a company logo, he or she will likely meet with company representatives to discuss such points as how and where the company is going to use the logo and what size, color, and shape preferences company executives might have. Project budgets must be respected. A design that may be perfect in every way but that is too costly to reproduce is basically useless. Graphic designers may need to compare their ideas with similar ones from other companies and analyze the image they project. They must have a good knowledge of how various colors, shapes, and layouts affect the viewer psychologically.

After a plan has been conceived and the details worked out, the graphic designer does some preliminary designs (generally two or three) to present to the client for approval. The client may reject the preliminary designs entirely and request a new one, or he or she may ask the designer to make alterations. The designer then goes back to the drawing board to attempt a new design or make the requested changes. This process continues until the client approves the design.

Once a design has been approved, the graphic designer prepares the piece for professional reproduction, or printing. The printer may require what is called a mechanical, in which the artwork and copy are arranged on a white board just as it is to be photographed, or the designer may be asked to submit an electronic copy of the design. Either way, designers must have a good understanding of the printing process, including color separation, paper properties, and halftone (photograph) reproduction.

REQUIREMENTS

High School
While in high school, take any art and design courses that are available. Computer classes are also helpful, particularly those that teach page layout programs or art and photography manipulation programs. Working on the school newspaper or yearbook can provide valuable design experience. You could also volunteer to design flyers or posters for school events.

Postsecondary Training
More graphic designers are recognizing the value of formal training; at least two out of three people entering the field today have a college degree or some college education. About 250 colleges and art

schools offer art and graphic design programs that are accredited by the National Association of Schools of Art and Design. At many schools, graphic design students must take a year of basic art and design courses before being accepted into the bachelor's degree program. In addition, applicants to the bachelor's degree programs in graphic arts may be asked to submit samples of their work to prove artistic ability. Many schools and employers depend on samples, or portfolios, to evaluate the applicants' skills in graphic design.

Many programs increasingly emphasize the importance of using computers for design work. Computer proficiency will be very important in the years to come. Interested individuals should select an academic program that incorporates computer training into the curriculum, or train themselves on their own.

A bachelor of fine arts program at a four-year college or university may include courses such as principles of design, art and art history, painting, sculpture, mechanical and architectural drawing, architecture, computer design, basic engineering, fashion designing and sketching, garment construction, and textiles. Such degrees are desirable but not always necessary for obtaining a position as a graphic designer.

Other Requirements

As with all artists, graphic designers need a degree of artistic talent, creativity, and imagination. They must be sensitive to beauty, have an eye for detail, and have a strong sense of color, balance, and proportion. Many of these qualities come naturally to potential graphic designers, but skills can be developed and improved through training, both on the job and in professional schools, colleges, and universities.

More and more graphic designers need solid computer skills and working knowledge of several of the common drawing, image editing, and page layout programs. Graphic design can be done on both Macintosh systems and on PCs; in fact, many designers have both types of computers in their studios.

With or without specialized education, graphic designers seeking employment should have a good portfolio containing samples of their best work. The graphic designer's portfolio is extremely important and can make a difference when an employer must choose between two otherwise equally qualified candidates.

A period of on-the-job training is expected for all beginning designers. The length of time it takes to become fully qualified as a graphic designer may run from one to three years, depending on prior education and experience, as well as innate talent.

EXPLORING

If you are interested in a career in graphic design, there are a number of ways to find out whether you have the talent, ambition, and perseverance to succeed in the field. Take as many art and design courses as possible while still in high school and become proficient at working on computers. To get an insider's view of various design occupations, you could enlist the help of art teachers or school guidance counselors to make arrangements to tour design firms and interview designers.

While in school, seek out practical experience by participating in school and community projects that call for design talents. These might include such activities as building sets for plays, setting up exhibits, planning seasonal and holiday displays, and preparing programs and other printed materials. If you are interested in publication design, work on the school newspaper or yearbook is invaluable.

Part-time and summer jobs are excellent ways to become familiar with the day-to-day requirements of a design job and gain some basic related experience. Possible places of employment include design studios, design departments in advertising agencies and manufacturing companies, department and furniture stores, flower shops, workshops that produce ornamental items, and museums. Museums also use a number of volunteer workers. Inexperienced people are often employed as sales, clerical, or general assistants; those with a little more education and experience may qualify for jobs in which they have a chance to develop actual design skills and build portfolios of completed design projects.

EMPLOYERS

Graphic designers in the advertising and marketing industries hold approximately 23,000 jobs in the United States. In addition to advertising and marketing, they work in many different industries, including the wholesale and retail trade (such as department stores, furniture and home furnishings stores, apparel stores, and florist shops); manufacturing industries (such as machinery, motor vehicles, aircraft, metal products, instruments, apparel, textiles, printing, and publishing); service industries (such as business services, engineering, and architecture); construction firms; and government agencies. Public relations and publicity firms, and mail-order houses all have graphic design departments. The publishing industry is a primary employer of graphic designers, including book publishers, magazines, newspapers, and newsletters.

About 25 percent of all graphic designers are self-employed, a higher proportion than is found in most other occupations. Freelance designers sell their services to multiple clients.

STARTING OUT

The best way to enter the field of graphic design is to have a strong portfolio. Potential employers rely on portfolios to evaluate talent and how that talent might be used to fit the company's needs. Beginning graphic designers can assemble a portfolio from work completed at school, in art classes, and in part-time or freelance jobs. The portfolio should continually be updated to reflect the designer's growing skills so it will always be ready for possible job changes.

Those just starting out can apply directly to companies that employ designers. Many colleges and professional schools have placement services to help graduates find positions, and sometimes it is possible to get a referral from a previous part-time employer or volunteer coordinator.

ADVANCEMENT

As part of their on-the-job training, beginning graphic designers generally are given simpler tasks and work under direct supervision. As they gain experience, they move up to more complex work with increasingly less supervision. Experienced graphic designers, especially those with leadership capabilities, may be promoted to chief designer, design department head, or other supervisory positions.

Graphic designers with strong computer skills can move into other computer-related positions with additional education. Some may become interested in graphics programming to further improve computer design capabilities. Others may want to become involved with multimedia and interactive graphics. Video games, touch-screen displays in stores, and even laser light shows are all products of multimedia graphic designers.

When designers develop personal styles that are in high demand in the marketplace, they sometimes go into business for themselves. Freelance design work can be erratic, however, so usually only the most experienced designers with an established client base can count on consistent full-time work.

EARNINGS

The range of salaries for graphic designers is quite broad. Many earn as little as $20,000, while others make more than $100,000. Salaries depend primarily on the nature and scope of the employer. The U.S. Department of Labor reports that in 2006, graphic designers employed in advertising and related services earned a mean salary of $45,590. Salaries for all graphic designers ranged from less than $24,120 to $69,730 or more.

The American Institute of Graphic Arts/Aquent Salary Survey 2007 reports that designers earned a median salary of $44,000, while senior designers earned a median of $60,000 annually. Salaried designers who advance to the position of creative/design director earned a median of $90,000 a year.

Self-employed designers can earn a lot one year and substantially more or less the next. Their earnings depend on individual talent and business ability, but, in general, are higher than those of salaried designers. Although like any self-employed individual, freelance designers must pay their own insurance costs and taxes and are not compensated for vacation or sick days.

Graphic designers who work for large corporations receive full benefits, including health insurance, paid vacation, and sick leave.

WORK ENVIRONMENT

Most graphic designers work regular hours in clean, comfortable, pleasant offices or studios. Conditions vary depending on the design specialty. Some graphic designers work in small establishments with few employees; others work in large organizations with large design departments. Some deal mostly with their coworkers; others may have a lot of public contact. Freelance designers are paid by the assignment. To maintain a steady income, they must constantly strive to please their clients and to find new ones. At times, graphic designers may have to work long, irregular hours to complete an especially ambitious project.

OUTLOOK

Employment for qualified graphic designers in the advertising and marketing industries is expected to grow much faster than the average for all occupations through 2016; employment should be especially strong for those involved with computer graphics and animation. As computer graphic and Web-based technology continues to advance, there will be a need for well-trained computer graphic designers. Companies that have always used graphic designers will expect their designers to perform work on computers. Companies for which graphic design was once too time consuming or costly are now sprucing up company newsletters and magazines, among other things, requiring the skills of design professionals.

Because the design field appeals to many talented individuals, competition is expected to be strong in all areas. Beginners and designers with only average talent or without formal education and technical skills may encounter some difficulty in finding a job.

FOR MORE INFORMATION

For profiles of advertising workers and career information, contact
Advertising Educational Foundation
220 East 42nd Street, Suite 3300
New York, NY 10017-5806
Tel: 212-986-8060
http://www.aef.com

For more information about careers in graphic design, contact
American Institute of Graphic Arts
164 Fifth Avenue
New York, NY 10010-5901
Tel: 212-807-1990
http://www.aiga.org

Visit the NASAD's Web site for information on schools.
National Association of Schools of Art and Design (NASAD)
11250 Roger Bacon Drive, Suite 21
Reston, VA 20190-5248
Tel: 703-437-0700
Email: info@arts-accredit.org
http://nasad.arts-accredit.org

For information on careers in environmental design, contact
Society for Environmental Graphic Design
1000 Vermont Avenue, Suite 400
Washington, DC 20005-4921
Tel: 202-638-5555
Email: segd@segd.org
http://www.segd.org

To read an online newsletter featuring competitions, examples of top designers' work, and industry news, visit the SPD's Web site.
Society of Publication Designers (SPD)
17 East 47th Street, 6th Floor
New York, NY 10017-1920
Tel: 212-223-3332
Email: mail@spd.org
http://www.spd.org

Illustrators

QUICK FACTS

School Subjects
Art
Computer science

Personal Skills
Artistic
Following instructions

Work Environment
Primarily indoors
Primarily one location

Minimum Education Level
High school diploma

Salary Range
$18,350 to $44,520 to
$79,390+

Certification or Licensing
None available

Outlook
Faster than the average

DOT
141

GOE
01.04.01

NOC
5241

O*NET-SOC
27-1013.00, 27-1013.01

OVERVIEW

Illustrators prepare drawings for advertisements, magazines, books, newspapers, packaging, Web sites, computer programs, and other formats.

HISTORY

The history of illustration can be traced back to the 8th century. Several famous illuminated manuscripts were created in the Middle Ages, including the *Book of Kells*. In the 15th century, movable type was introduced and came to be used by book illustrators. Other printing methods such as etching, woodcuts, and copper engravings were used as illustration techniques in the 16th century and beyond.

In 1796, lithography was invented in Germany. In the original process of lithography, artists made prints directly from designs drawn on slabs of stone. Metal sheets eventually replaced these stone slabs. By the mid-1800s, illustrators used lithographs and engravings to draw magazine and newspaper pages.

As knowledge of photography developed and advanced reproduction processes were invented, artists increasingly used photographs as illustrations. Many industries today, ranging from advertising to fashion, employ illustrators.

THE JOB

Illustrators create artwork for both commercial and fine art purposes. They use a variety of media—pencil, pen and ink, pastels, paints (oil, acrylic, and watercolor), airbrush, collage, and computer technology. Illustrations are used to decorate, describe, inform, clarify, instruct, and draw attention. They appear everywhere in print and electronic formats, including books, magazines, newspapers, signs and billboards, packaging (for everything from milk cartons to CDs), Web sites, computer programs, greeting cards, calendars, stationery, and direct mail.

Illustrators often work as part of a creative team, which can include graphic designers, photographers, and individuals who draw lettering called *calligraphers.* Illustrators work in almost every industry. Fashion illustration is one of the fastest growing specialties.

Fashion illustrators work in a glamorized, intense environment. Their artistic focus is specifically on styles of clothing and personal image. Illustrators can work in a few different categories of the fashion field. They provide artwork to accompany editorial pieces in magazines such as *Glamour, Redbook,* and *Vogue* and newspapers such as *Women's Wear Daily.* Catalog companies employ fashion illustrators to provide the artwork that sells their merchandise.

Fashion illustrators also work with fashion designers, editors, and models. They make sketches from designers' notes or they may sketch live models during runway shows or other fashion presentations. They may use pencils, pen and ink, charcoal, paint, or a combination of media. Fashion illustrators may work as freelancers, handling all the business aspects that go along with being self-employed.

Medical illustrators, with special training in biology and the physical sciences, draw accurate illustrations of parts of the human body, animals, and plants.

Natural science illustrators create illustrations of plants and wildlife. They often work at museums such as the Smithsonian Institution.

Children's book illustrators specialize in creating artwork for books and other publications for young people.

REQUIREMENTS

High School
Creative talent is more important in this field than education. However, there are academic programs in illustration at most colleges and universities. If you are considering going on to a formal program, take plenty of art classes while in high school. Elective classes in ceramics, illustration, painting, or photography are common courses offered at many high schools.

Postsecondary Training

To find a salaried position as a general illustrator, you should have at least a high school diploma and preferably an associate's or bachelor's degree in commercial art or fine art. Whether you are looking for full-time employment or freelance assignments, you will need an organized collection of samples of your best work, which is called a portfolio. Employers are especially interested in work that has been published or printed. An advantage to pursuing education beyond high school is that it gives you an opportunity to build your portfolio.

Fashion illustrators should study clothing construction, fashion design, and cosmetology in addition to taking art courses. They should also keep up with the latest fashion and illustration trends by reading fashion magazines.

Certification or Licensing

Illustrators need to continue their education and training while pursuing their careers. Licensing and certification are not required in this field. However, illustrators must keep up with the latest innovations in design techniques, computer software, and presentation technology, as well as technological advances in the fields for which they provide illustrations.

Other Requirements

Illustrators must be creative, and, of course, demonstrate artistic talent and skill. They also need to be flexible. Because their art is often commercial in nature, illustrators must be willing to accommodate their employers' desires if they are to build a broad clientele and earn a decent living. They must be able to take suggestions and rejections gracefully.

EXPLORING

You can explore an interest in this career by taking art courses. Artists can always improve their drawing skills by practicing on their own, either producing original artwork, or making sketches from drawings that appear in textbooks and reference manuals that relate to their interests. Participation in art, science, and fashion clubs is also good exposure.

EMPLOYERS

Approximately 62 percent of all visual artists are self-employed. Illustrators who are not self-employed work in advertising and marketing agencies, design firms, commercial art and reproduction firms, or printing and publishing firms. They are also employed in the motion picture and television industries, wholesale and retail trade establishments, and public relations firms. Fashion illustrators are employed at magazines, newspapers, and catalog companies.

STARTING OUT

Graduates of illustration programs should develop a portfolio of their work to show to prospective employers or clients. Most schools offer career counseling and job placement assistance to their graduates. Job ads and employment agencies are also potential sources for locating work.

ADVANCEMENT

After an illustrator gains experience, he or she will be given more challenging and unusual work. Those with strong computer skills will have the best chances for advancement. Illustrators can advance by developing skills in a specialized area, or even starting their own business. Illustrators can also go into teaching, in colleges and universities at the undergraduate and graduate levels.

EARNINGS

The pay for illustrations can be as little as a byline, though in the beginning of your career it may be worth it just to get exposure. Some illustrators can earn several thousand dollars for a single illustration. Freelance work is often uncertain because of the fluctuation in pay rates and steadiness of assignments. The U.S. Department of Labor reports that median earnings for salaried fine artists (including painters, sculptors, and illustrators) employed in the advertising industry were $44,520 a year in 2006. Salaries for all fine artists ranged from less than $18,350 to $79,390 or more.

Illustrators generally receive good benefits, including health and life insurance, pension plans, and vacation, sick, and holiday pay. Self-employed illustrators must provide their own benefits.

WORK ENVIRONMENT

Illustrators generally work in clean, well-lit offices. They spend a great deal of time at their desks, whether in front of a computer or at the drafting table. Fashion illustrators may be required to attend fashion shows and other industry events. Because the fashion world is extremely competitive and fast paced, fashion illustrators tend to work long hours under the pressure of deadlines and demanding personalities.

OUTLOOK

Employment of visual artists is expected to grow faster than the average for all occupations through 2016, according to the *Occupational Outlook Handbook*. The growth of the Internet should provide opportunities for illustrators, although the increased use of computer-aided design systems is a threat because individuals do not necessarily need artistic talent or training to use them. Illustrators employed in the advertising and marketing industries should also have strong employment prospects.

The outlook for careers in fashion illustration is dependent on the businesses of magazine publishing and advertising. Growth of advertising and public relations agencies will provide new jobs. The popularity of American fashion in other parts of the world will also create a demand for fashion illustrators to provide the artwork needed to sell to a global market.

FOR MORE INFORMATION

For profiles of advertising workers and career information, contact
Advertising Educational Foundation
220 East 42nd Street, Suite 3300
New York, NY 10017-5806
Tel: 212-986-8060
http://www.aef.com

This organization is committed to improving conditions for all creators of graphic art and to raising standards for the entire industry. For information, contact
Graphic Artists Guild
32 Broadway, Suite 1114
New York, NY 10004-1612
Tel: 212-791-3400
http://www.gag.org

For information on education programs, contact
National Association of Schools of Art and Design
11250 Roger Bacon Drive, Suite 21
Reston, VA 20190-5248

Tel: 703-437-0700
Email: info@arts-accredit.org
http://nasad.arts-accredit.org

This organization promotes and stimulates interest in the art of illustration by offering exhibits, lectures, educational programs, and social exchange. For information, contact
Society of Illustrators
128 East 63rd Street
New York, NY 10021-7303
Tel: 212-838-2560
Email: info@societyillustrators.org
http://www.societyillustrators.org

INTERVIEW

Wally Littman is a freelance illustrator in Teaneck, New Jersey. (Visit http://www.wallylittmanillustrator.com to view his work.) He has created illustrations for the advertising industry, comic books, newspapers, magazines, and many other fields. Wally discussed his career with the editors of Careers in Focus: Advertising and Marketing.

Q. Why did you decide to become an illustrator?

A. I feel that humor is the best medicine for an ailing world. It also is an ideal way to make a serious subject more palatable.

Q. How long have you been an illustrator? Tell us about your work.

A. I was doing cartoons in grade school. I sold my first gag cartoon at 16. After high school I got a job as a comic book editor and did filler pages for them.

Then I got drafted. The army felt that I would be a better combat engineer than a cartoonist. I planted booby traps and laid minefields in Korea for nearly two years. After my discharge I enrolled in Pratt Institute. I majored in advertising design and illustration. I eventually went into advertising so I could support my new family; 48 years later, I finally became a full-time gag cartoonist. A dream come true.

Q. What do you like most about your job?

A. Being a freelancer allows me to regulate my time. When I go on vacation, I send cartoon postcards to my clients telling them that I'll need more work when I return.

Q. What are the most key components of a quality piece of advertising illustration?

A. There is no simple answer to this question. The illustration has to accomplish, as simply as possible, what the concept of the ad is. Technique should be secondary: Concept is king!

Q. What advice would you give to high school students who are interested in this career?

A. The best advice I could give to any student is:

- Get a good education.
- Never give up.
- Work your tail off.
- Never give up.
- Network. Join clubs and associations that are involved in your field.
- Never give up.
- Keep in touch with your peers.

Internet Marketing and Advertising Consultants

OVERVIEW

Internet marketing and advertising consultants use their business savvy and technological and computer skills to help companies promote their services or products on the Internet. This method is often referred to as e-marketing. Some larger companies may have an in-house staff of Internet professionals, though many smaller or start-up companies often turn to independent consultants or a consulting agency for their needs.

HISTORY

The modern Internet as we know it has only been around less than two decades. In this short amount of time, the Internet has brought new ways of communicating, marketing, and selling products and services to customers, without the presence of an actual store or office. With the fast growth of Internet sales and services, companies with a Web presence sought people who could create online advertising and marketing campaigns to reach customers. This created the need for the Internet advertising and marketing consultant. Because of constantly evolving technology, the future will require even more specialized and complex skills of Internet marketing and advertising consultants.

Some consultants belong to the Search Engine Marketing Professional Organization, an international nonprofit group founded in 2003.

THE JOB

While the work of Internet marketing and advertising consultants can vary depending on their place of employment and the project at hand, they all work toward the same goal: to drive more traffic to a company's Web site and sell more products or services.

The first step for many Internet marketing projects is revising or creating a company's Web site. If the Web site already exists, Internet marketing and advertising consultants study it to ensure that it is an effective marketing tool for the company's products or services. They might ask the following questions: Is the site attractive to potential customers? Is it is easy to navigate? Is there enough information available about the products or services? Is purchasing a product easy? Are there any features that may deter customers from completing a purchase? How does the site compare to those of competitors? Once these questions are answered, the consultants revise and revamp the Web site to make it a more effective marketing tool.

Internet marketing and advertising consultants may also be tasked with creating a brand-new Web site for a company that is new to the Web. To do this, they need to consider the company's marketing goals, design elements, user interface, purchasing interface, and the actual products or services that will be marketed. Internet consultants may collaborate with a team of artists, art directors, photographers, graphic designers, stylists, and copywriters to gather images and create merchandise presentations and product descriptions that stay true to the retail's brand.

In addition, marketing and advertising consultants are responsible for implementing an e-commerce strategy that addresses concerns such as retail competition, special promotions, and the overall performance of the site. They must identify the company's potential market (teens, Hispanic males, seniors, etc.), customer's expectations regarding a Web site (state-of-the-art graphics and vivid colors, quick-loading pages, a straightforward, conservative look, etc.), and customer's buying habits. Customers who shop online typically have very different buying habits than those who purchase products in brick-and-mortar stores. For example, a customer who shops online might like the immediacy of being able to shop at home, but may also be seeking quick delivery options or a large selection of products from which to choose. Others may use the Web site to conduct research, but follow up by purchasing the product on the telephone or by visiting a brick-and-mortar store.

Many Internet marketing and advertising consultants specialize in different areas of the industry. For example, *search engine marketers* (*SEMs*) are responsible for the day-to-day management of clients' Web sites. They research a client's products or services, and develop advertisements using concise descriptions and keywords that will place their company's Web site high in search rankings. SEMs optimize ad campaigns with the most effective keywords so potential consumers are directed to the client's Web site during a search—the ultimate goal is to be listed as high as possible in a search engine's top 10 results.

Others work as *pay per click specialists (PPCs)*. PPCs place, or imbed, a client's advertisement on an existing Web site, often in the form of an image or banner. PPCs research sites, or content providers, that have an interest or relation to their client's business. For example, a PPC representing clients who sell vitamin supplements, health club memberships, or energy drinks may contact the online manager of an exercise Web site to convince him or her to place banner ads or sponsored links at the site. Clicking on these banners or links will direct the user to the advertiser's Web site. PPCs regularly monitor logfiles to determine the number of visits or "clicks," and then pay the content provider accordingly.

REQUIREMENTS

High School
If you are considering a career as an Internet marketing and advertising consultant, you should pursue a general high school curriculum that is college preparatory. Make sure you enroll in advertising, business, computer science, and marketing courses. You should also take courses that develop your analytical and problem-solving skills such as mathematics (including algebra and geometry) and sciences (including chemistry and physics). Take English courses to develop the research and communication skills you'll need for this profession.

Postsecondary Training
While a college degree may not be necessary to gain entry into this field, you will find it easier to get the best jobs and advance if you have one. Some people enter the field with computer- or e-commerce-related degrees; others have traditional liberal arts, advertising, business, or marketing backgrounds that include computer studies. No matter what your major, take plenty of computer classes and spend a lot of time on the Web.

Because consultants are usually responsible for marketing themselves, you should have good business skills and knowledge of marketing and sales, as well as computer knowledge. Therefore, take business and management classes, as well as economics and marketing. The consultant with a broad educational background may have the inside edge in certain situations.

Other Requirements

Marketing and advertising consultants must be lifelong learners. You should have the desire and initiative to keep up on new technology, software, and hardware, as well as new marketing and advertising techniques. You must also have good communication skills, including good listening skills. Creativity and a good eye for graphic design are also desirable. Because marketing and advertising consultants deal with many different people in various lines of work, you must be flexible and have good interpersonal skills. To be a successful consultant, you should be self-motivated and have the ability to work alone as well as with groups. You also need to have the patience and perseverance to see projects through.

EXPLORING

By simply accessing the Internet frequently and observing different Web site designs, marketing techniques, and the increasing number of e-commerce sites, you can gain an insight into the field. Contact advertising and marketing workers, computer consultants, or Web site designers in your area and set up an information interview. At the interview ask them questions about their educational background, what they like about the work, how they market their business, what important skills someone wanting to enter the field should have, and any other things you are interested in knowing about this work.

Obtain experience in advertising and marketing by working on your school newspaper or yearbook or by finding a part-time or summer job at an advertising or marketing firm (especially one that specializes in Internet marketing/advertising). You can also create an online advertising or marketing campaign for a real or imaginary product or service.

EMPLOYERS

Many marketing and advertising consultants work independently, running their own consulting businesses. Others may be salaried employees of traditional management consulting firms that have Internet marketing/advertising consulting divisions or departments. And still others may work for traditional brick-and-mortar companies that have a strong presence on the Internet.

Independent consultants have the added responsibility of marketing their services and always looking for new projects. Consultants at a firm are typically assigned to work on certain projects.

Clients that hire marketing and advertising consultants include small businesses, large corporations, and government institutions. Consultants work all across the country (and world), but large cities may offer more job opportunities. Some consultants specialize in working with a certain type of business such as department stores or computer companies.

STARTING OUT

Most consultants enter the field by working for an established consulting firm. This way they can gain experience and develop a portfolio and a list of references before venturing out on their own as an independent consultant or moving to a different firm in a higher position. The Internet is a good resource to use to find employment. Many sites post job openings. Local employment agencies and newspapers and trade magazines also list job opportunities. In addition, your college's career services office should be able to help you.

Networking is a key element to becoming a successful consultant and requires getting in touch with previous business and social associates as well as making new contacts.

ADVANCEMENT

Internet marketing and advertising consultants have several avenues for advancement. As they become known as experts in their field, the demand for their services will increase. This demand can support an increase in fees. They can also specialize in a certain segment of the industry, which can increase their client base and fees. Those working for consulting firms may move into management or partner positions. Consultants who want to work independently can advance by starting their own businesses. Eventually they may be able to hire consultants to work under them. Because of the continuous developments within the information technology industry, advancement possibilities for consultants who continually upgrade their knowledge and skills are practically endless.

EARNINGS

Internet marketing and advertising consultants' earnings vary widely depending on their geographic location, type of company they work for, and their experience and reputation. Beginning consultants may make about $35,000 per year, while many consultants earn around $65,000 annually. Some consultants have salaries that exceed $100,000 a year.

Search engine marketers earn annual salaries that range from $30,000 to $100,000 or more, according to the Search Engine Marketing Professional Organization.

Many independent consultants charge by the hour, with fees ranging from $45 to well above $100 an hour. Consultants who work on contract must estimate the hours needed to complete the project and their rate of pay when determining their contract price. Independent consultants must also realize that not all their work time is "billable," meaning that time spent on general office work, record keeping, billing, maintaining current client contacts, and seeking new business does not generate revenue. This nonbillable time must be factored into contract or hourly rates when determining annual income.

Although independent consultants may generate good contract or hourly fees, they do not receive benefits that may be typical of salaried employees. For example, independent consultants are responsible for their own medical, disability, and life insurance. They do not receive vacation pay, and when they are not working, they are not generating income. Retirement plans must also be self-funded and self-directed.

WORK ENVIRONMENT

Internet marketing and advertising consultants work in a variety of settings. Depending on the project, they may work out of their homes or private offices. At other times, they may be required to work on-site at the client's facilities, which may, for example, be an office building or factory. Consultants employed by a large or small consulting firm or as full-time employees may also spend time working at the organization's office or telecommuting from home.

Internet consultants generally can expect to work in a clean office environment. Consultants may work independently or as part of a team, depending on the project's requirements.

Consulting can be a very intense job that may require long hours to meet a project's deadline. Some settings where employees or consultants are driven by a strict deadline or where a project is not progressing as planned may be stressful. Many people in this field often work more than 40 hours a week and may need to work nights and weekends. In addition, Internet consultants must spend time keeping current with the latest technology and marketing and advertising techniques by reading and researching.

OUTLOOK

There is currently a large demand for Internet marketing and advertising consultants as a result of the rapid growth of Internet sales. Consultants who keep current with technology and industry trends and who are willing to learn and adapt should have plenty of job opportunities.

FOR MORE INFORMATION

For profiles of advertising workers and career information, contact
Advertising Educational Foundation
220 East 42nd Street, Suite 3300
New York, NY 10017-5806
Tel: 212-986-8060
http://www.aef.com

The AAF combines the mutual interests of corporate advertisers, agencies, media companies, suppliers, and academia. Visit its Web site to learn more about internships, scholarships, student chapters, and awards.
American Advertising Federation (AAF)
1101 Vermont Avenue, NW, Suite 500
Washington, DC 20005-6306
Tel: 800-999-2231
Email: aaf@aaf.org
http://www.aaf.org

For industry information, contact
American Association of Advertising Agencies
405 Lexington Avenue, 18th Floor
New York, NY 10174-1801
Tel: 212-682-2500
http://www.aaaa.org

For information on the practice, study, and teaching of marketing, contact
American Marketing Association
311 South Wacker Drive, Suite 5800
Chicago, IL 60606-6629

Tel: 800-AMA-1150
http://www.marketingpower.com

For information on search engine marketing, contact
Search Engine Marketing Professional Organization
401 Edgewater Place, Suite 600
Wakefield, MA 01880-6200
http://www.sempo.org

Marketing Research Analysts

OVERVIEW

Marketing research analysts collect, analyze, and interpret data to determine potential demand for a product or service. By examining the buying habits, wants, needs, and preferences of consumers, research analysts are able to recommend ways to improve products, increase sales, and expand customer bases. There are approximately 7,000 marketing research analysts employed in advertising and related industries in the United States.

HISTORY

Knowing what customers want and what prices they are willing to pay have always been concerns of manufacturers and producers of goods and services. As industries have grown and competition for consumers of manufactured goods has increased, businesses have turned to marketing research as a way to measure public opinion and assess customer preferences.

Marketing research formally emerged in Germany in the 1920s and in Sweden and France in the 1930s. In the United States, emphasis on marketing research began after World War II. With a desire to study potential markets and gain new customers, U.S. firms hired marketing research specialists, professionals who were able to use statistics and refine research techniques to help companies reach their marketing goals. By the 1980s, research analysts could be found even in Communist countries, where the quantity of consumer goods being produced was rapidly increasing.

Today, the marketing research analyst is a vital part of the marketing team. By conducting studies and analyzing data, research professionals help companies address specific marketing issues and concerns.

THE JOB

Marketing researchers collect and analyze all kinds of information to help companies improve their products, establish or modify sales and distribution policies, and make decisions regarding future plans and directions. In addition, research analysts are responsible for monitoring both in-house studies and off-site research, interpreting results, providing explanations of compiled data, and developing research tools.

One area of marketing research focuses on company products and services. To determine consumer likes and dislikes, research analysts collect data on brand names, trademarks, product design, and packaging for existing products, items being test-marketed, and those in experimental stages. Analysts also study competing products and services that are already on the market to help managers and strategic planners develop new products and create appropriate advertising campaigns.

In the sales methods and policy area of marketing research, analysts examine firms' sales records and conduct a variety of sales-related studies. For example, information on sales in various geographical areas is analyzed and compared to previous sales figures, changes in population, and total and seasonal sales volume. By analyzing this data, marketing researchers can identify peak sales periods and recommend ways to target new customers. Such information helps marketers plan future sales campaigns and establish sales quotas and commissions.

Advertising research is closely related to sales research. Studies on the effectiveness of advertising in different parts of the country are conducted and compared to sales records. This research is helpful in planning future advertising campaigns and in selecting the appropriate media to use.

Marketing research that focuses on consumer demand and preferences solicits opinions of the people who use the products or services being considered. In addition to actually conducting opinion studies, marketing researchers often design the ways to obtain the information. They write scripts for telephone interviews, develop direct mail questionnaires and field surveys, and devise focus group programs.

Through one or a combination of these studies, market researchers gather information on consumer reaction to the need for and style, design, price, and use of a product. The studies attempt to reveal who uses various products or services, identify potential customers, or get suggestions for product or service improvement. This information is helpful for forecasting sales, planning design modifications, and determining changes in features.

Once information has been gathered, marketing researchers analyze the results. They then detail their findings and recommendations in a written report and often orally present them to management as well.

A number of professionals compose the marketing research team. The *project supervisor* is responsible for overseeing a study from beginning to end. The *statistician* determines the sample size—or the number of people to be surveyed—and compares the number of responses. The project supervisor or statistician, in conjunction with other specialists (such as *demographers* and *psychologists*), often determines the number of interviews to be conducted as well as their locations. *Field interviewers* survey people in various public places, such as shopping malls, office complexes, and popular attractions. *Telemarketers* gather information by placing calls to current or potential customers, to people listed in telephone books, or to those who appear on specialized lists obtained from list houses. Once questionnaires come in from the field, *tabulators* and *coders* examine the data, count the answers, code noncategorical answers, and tally the primary counts. The marketing research analyst then analyzes the returns, writes up the final report, and makes recommendations to the client or to management.

Marketing research analysts must be thoroughly familiar with research techniques and procedures. Sometimes the research problem is clearly defined, and information can be gathered readily. Other times, company executives may know only that a problem exists as evidenced by a decline in sales. In these cases, the market research analyst is expected to collect the facts that will aid in revealing and resolving the problem.

REQUIREMENTS

High School

Most employers require their marketing research analysts to hold at least a bachelor's degree, so a college preparatory program is advised. Classes in economics, English, marketing, mathematics, psychology, and sociology are particularly important. Courses in computing are especially useful, since a great deal of tabulation and statistical analysis is required in the marketing research field.

Postsecondary Training

A bachelor's degree is essential for careers in marketing research. Majors in business administration, computer science, economics, history, marketing, or statistics provide a good background for most types of research positions. In addition, course work in psychology and sociology is helpful for those who are leaning toward consumer demand and opinion research. Since quantitative skills are important in various types of industrial or analytic research, students interested in these areas should take econometrics, sampling theory, statistics, survey design, and other mathematics courses.

Many employers prefer that a marketing research analyst hold a bachelor's as well as a master's degree. A master's of business administration, for example, is frequently required on projects calling for complex statistical and business analysis. Graduate work at the doctorate level is not necessary for most positions, but it is highly desirable for those who plan to become involved in advanced research studies.

Certification and Licensing

The Marketing Research Association offers certification for marketing research analysts. Contact the association for more information.

Other Requirements

To work in this career, you should be intelligent, detail oriented, and accurate; have the ability to work easily with words and numbers; and be particularly interested in solving problems through data collection and analysis. In addition, you must be patient and persistent, since long hours are often required when working on complex studies.

As part of the market research team, you must be able to work well with others and have an interest in people. The ability to communicate, both orally and in writing, is also important, since you will be responsible for writing detailed reports on the findings in various studies and presenting recommendations to management.

EXPLORING

You can find many opportunities in high school to learn more about the necessary skills for the field of marketing research. For example, experiments in science, problems in student government, committee work, and other school activities provide exposure to situations similar to those encountered by marketing research analysts.

You can also seek part-time employment as a survey interviewer at local marketing research firms. Gathering field data for consumer surveys offers valuable experience through actual contact with both the public and marketing research supervisors. In addition, many companies seek a variety of other employees to code, tabulate, and edit surveys; monitor telephone interviews; and validate the information entered on written questionnaires. You can search for job listings in local newspapers and on the Web or apply directly to research organizations.

EMPLOYERS

Approximately 7,000 marketing research analysts are employed in advertising and related industries in the United States. Marketing research analysts are also employed by large corporations, industrial firms, marketing agencies, data collection businesses, and private research organizations that handle local surveys for companies on a contract basis. While many marketing research organizations offer a broad range of services, some firms subcontract parts of an overall project to specialized companies. For example, one research firm may concentrate on product interviews, while another might focus on measuring the effectiveness of product advertising. Similarly, some marketing analysts specialize in one industry or area. For instance, agricultural marketing specialists prepare sales forecasts for food businesses, which use the information in their advertising and sales programs.

Although many smaller firms located all across the country outsource studies to marketing research firms, these agencies, along with most large corporations that employ marketing research analysts, are located in such big cities as Chicago and New York. Approximately 90 percent of salaried marketing research analysts are employed in private industry, but opportunities also exist in government and academia, as well as at hospitals, public libraries, and a variety of other types of organizations.

STARTING OUT

Students with a graduate degree in marketing research and experience in quantitative techniques have the best chances of landing jobs as marketing research analysts. Since a bachelor's degree in marketing or business is usually not sufficient to obtain such a position, many employees without postgraduate degrees start out as research assistants, trainees, interviewers, or questionnaire editors. In such positions, those aspiring to the job of research analyst can gain valuable experience conducting interviews, analyzing data, and writing reports.

Use your college career services office, the Web, and help wanted sections of local newspapers to look for job leads. Another way to gain entry into the marketing research field is through personal and professional contacts. Names and telephone numbers of potential employers may come from professors, friends, or relatives. Finally, students who have participated in internships or have held marketing research-related jobs on a part-time basis while in school or during the summer may be able to obtain employment at these firms or at similar organizations.

ADVANCEMENT

Most marketing research professionals begin as *junior analysts* or *research assistants*. In these positions, they help prepare question-naires and related materials, train survey interviewers, and tabulate and code survey results. After gaining sufficient experience in these and other aspects of research project development, employees are often assigned their own research projects, which usually involve supervisory and planning responsibilities. A typical promotion path for those climbing the company ladder might be from assistant researcher to marketing research analyst to assistant manager and then to manager of a branch office for a large private research firm. From there, some professionals become market research executives or research directors for industrial or business firms.

Since marketing research analysts learn about all aspects of marketing on the job, some advance by moving to positions in other departments, such as advertising or sales. Depending on the interests and experience of marketing professionals, other areas of employment to which they can advance include data processing, teaching at the university level, statistics, economics, and industrial research and development.

In general, few employees go from starting positions to executive jobs at one company. Advancement often requires changing employers. Therefore, marketing research analysts who want to move up the ranks frequently go from one company to another, sometimes many times during their careers.

EARNINGS

Beginning salaries in marketing research depend on the qualifications of the employee, nature of the position, and size of the firm. Interviewers, coders, tabulators, editors, and a variety of other employees usually get paid by the hour and may start at $6 or more per hour. The U.S. Department of Labor reported that in 2006, median annual earnings of market research analysts were $58,820. The middle 50 percent earned salaries that ranged from $42,190 to $84,070. Salaries ranged from less than $32,250 to more than $112,510. Experienced analysts working in supervisory positions at large firms can earn even higher earnings. Market research directors earn up to $200,000.

Because most marketing research workers are employed by business or industrial firms, they receive typical fringe benefit packages, including health and life insurance, pension plans, and paid vacation and sick leave.

WORK ENVIRONMENT

Marketing research analysts usually work a 40-hour week. Occasionally, overtime is necessary to meet project deadlines. Although they frequently interact with a variety of marketing research team members, analysts also do a lot of independent work, analyzing data, writing reports, and preparing statistical charts.

While most marketing research analysts work in offices located at the firm's main headquarters, those who supervise interviewers may go into the field to oversee work. Many market research analysts find that regular travel is required to attend conferences, meet with clients, or check on the progress of various research studies.

OUTLOOK

The U.S. Department of Labor predicts that employment for marketing research analysts in the advertising and marketing industries will grow much faster than the average for all occupations through 2016. Increasing competition among producers of consumer goods and services and industrial products, combined with a growing awareness of the value of marketing research data, will contribute to opportunities in the field. Overall, opportunities will be best for those with graduate degrees who seek employment in marketing research firms, companies that design computer systems and software, financial services organizations, health care institutions, advertising firms, manufacturing firms that produce consumer goods, and insurance companies.

While many new graduates are attracted to the field, creating a competitive situation, the best jobs and the highest pay will go to those individuals who hold a master's degree or doctorate in computer science, economics, marketing research, or statistics.

FOR MORE INFORMATION

For information on college chapters, internship opportunities, and financial aid opportunities, contact
American Advertising Federation
1101 Vermont Avenue, NW, Suite 500
Washington, DC 20005-6306
Tel: 800-999-2231
Email: aaf@aaf.org
http://www.aaf.org

For information on graduate programs, contact
American Association for Public Opinion Research
PO Box 14263
Lenexa, KS 66285-4263
Tel: 913-895-4601
Email: info@aapor.org
http://www.aapor.org

For information on advertising agencies, contact
American Association of Advertising Agencies
405 Lexington Avenue, 18th Floor
New York, NY 10174-1801
Tel: 212-682-2500
http://www.aaaa.org

For career resources and job listings, contact
American Marketing Association
311 South Wacker Drive, Suite 5800
Chicago, IL 60606-6629
Tel: 800-262-1150
http://www.marketingpower.com

For comprehensive information on market and opinion research, contact
Council for Marketing and Opinion Research
110 National Drive, 2nd Floor
Glastonbury, CT 06033-1212
Tel: 860-657-1881
Email: information@cmor.org
http://www.cmor.org

For information on graduate programs in marketing, contact
Council of American Survey Research Organizations
170 North Country Road, Suite 4
Port Jefferson, NY 11777-2606
Tel: 631-928-6954
Email: casro@casro.org
http://www.casro.org

For information on education and training, contact
Marketing Research Association
110 National Drive, 2nd Floor
Glastonbury, CT 06033-1212
Tel: 860-682-1000
Email: email@mra-net.org
http://www.mra-net.org

For career information, visit
Careers Outside the Box: Survey Research: A Fun, Exciting, Rewarding Career
http://www.casro.org/careers

Media Planners and Buyers

QUICK FACTS

School Subjects
Business
English
Speech

Personal Skills
Artistic
Communication/ideas

Work Environment
Primarily indoors
One location with some
  travel

Minimum Education Level
Bachelor's degree

Salary Range
$25,000 to $50,000 to
$130,000+

Certification or Licensing
None available

Outlook
Faster than the average

DOT
162

GOE
10.02.02, 13.02.02

NOC
1225

O*NET-SOC
41-3011.00

OVERVIEW

Media specialists are responsible for placing advertisements that will reach targeted customers and get the best response from the market for the least amount of money. Typically, these advertisements are for products or services, but other advertisements might seek to influence public opinion regarding a controversial issue, provide information to the public about a cause or event, or attract interest in an organization. For example, an electric company might purchase a newspaper ad to defend its recent rate hike; a charity might buy a 30-second advertisement on public radio to educate people about the plight of refugees in Sudan; or the U.S. Navy might purchase an ad in a popular teen magazine to reach potential recruits.

Within the media department, *media planners* gather information about the sizes and types of audiences that can be reached through each of the various media and about the cost of advertising in each medium. *Media buyers,* sometimes called *advertising sales agents,* purchase space in printed publications, as well as time on radio or television stations. Media workers are supervised by a *media director,* who is accountable for the overall media plan. In addition to advertising agencies, media planners and buyers work for large companies that purchase space or broadcast time. There are approximately 51,000 advertising sales agents employed in the advertising industry and related fields in the United States.

112

HISTORY

The first formal media that allowed advertisers to deliver messages about their products or services to the public were newspapers and magazines, which began selling space to advertisers in the late 19th century. This system of placing ads gave rise to the first media planners and buyers, who were in charge of deciding what kind of advertising to put in which publications and then actually purchasing the space.

In the broadcast realm, radio stations started offering program time to advertisers in the early 1900s. And, while television advertising began just before the end of World War II, producers were quick to realize that they could reach huge audiences by placing ads on TV. Television advertising proved to be beneficial to the TV stations as well, since they relied on sponsors for financial assistance to bring programs into people's homes. In the past, programs were sometimes named not for the host or star of the program, but for the sponsoring company that was paying for the broadcast of that particular show.

During the early years of radio and television, it was often possible for one sponsor to pay for an entire 30-minute program. The cost of producing shows on radio and television, however, increased dramatically, requiring many sponsors to support a single radio or television program. Media planners and buyers learned to get more for their money by buying smaller amounts of time—60-, 30-, and even 10-second spots—on a greater number of programs.

Today's media planners and buyers have a wide array of media from which to choose. The newest of these, the World Wide Web, allows advertisers not only to precisely target customers, but to interact with them as well. In addition to Web banner ads, producers can also advertise via sponsorships, their own Web sites, CD catalogs, and more. With so many choices, media planners and buyers must carefully determine target markets and select the ideal media mix to reach these markets at the least cost.

THE JOB

While many employees may work in the media department, the primary specialists are the media planner and the media buyer. They work with professionals from a wide range of media—from billboards, direct mail, and newspapers and magazines to television, radio, and the Internet. Both types of media specialists must be familiar with the markets that each medium reaches, as well as the advantages and disadvantages of advertising in each.

Media planners determine target markets based on their clients' advertising or public relations (PR) needs. Considering their clients' products and services or PR goal, budget, and image, media planners gather information about the public's viewing, reading, and buying habits by administering questionnaires and conducting other forms of market research. Through this research, planners are able to identify target markets by sorting data according to people's ages, incomes, marital status, interests, and leisure activities.

By knowing which groups of people watch certain shows, listen to specific radio stations, or read particular magazines or newspapers, media planners can help clients select air time or print space to reach the consumers most likely to buy their products or be interested in the information that is being conveyed. For example, people who care about protecting the environment typically subscribe to environmentally focused magazines such as *Sierra*. Media planners will recommend that an ecotourism company purchase print space in the magazine to reach potential customers.

Media planners who work directly for companies selling air time or print space must be sensitive to their clients' budgets and resources. When tailoring their sales pitch to a particular client's needs, planners often go to great lengths to persuade the client to buy air time or advertising space. They produce brochures and reports that detail the characteristics of their viewing or reading market, including the average income of those individuals, the number of people who see the ads, and any other information that may be likely to encourage potential advertisers to promote their products.

Media planners try to land contracts by inviting clients to meetings and presentations and educating them about various marketing strategies. They must not only pursue new clients but also attend to current ones, making sure that they are happy with their existing advertising packages. For both new and existing clients, the media planner's main objective is to sell as much air time or ad space as possible.

Media buyers do the actual purchasing of the time on radio or television or the space in a newspaper or magazine in which an advertisement will run. In addition to tracking the time and space available for purchase, media buyers ensure that ads appear when and where they should, negotiate costs for ad placement, and calculate rates, usage, and budgets. They are also responsible for maintaining contact with clients, keeping them informed of all advertising-related developments and resolving any conflicts that arise. Large companies that generate a lot of advertising or those that place only print ads or only broadcast ads sometimes differentiate between the two main media groups by employing *space buyers* and/or *time buyers*.

Workers who actually sell the print space or air time to advertisers are called *print sales workers* or *broadcast time salespeople*. Like media planners, these professionals are well versed about the target markets served by their organizations and can often provide useful information about editorial content or broadcast programs.

In contrast to print and broadcast planners and buyers, *interactive media specialists* are responsible for managing all critical aspects of their clients' online advertising campaigns. While interactive media planners may have responsibilities similar to those of print or broadcast planners, they also act as new technology specialists, placing and tracking all online ads and maintaining relationships with clients and Webmasters alike.

The typical online media planning process begins with an agency spreadsheet that details the criteria about the media buy. These criteria often include target demographics, start and end dates for the ad campaign, and online objectives. After sending all relevant information to a variety of Web sites, the media specialist receives cost, market, and other data from the sites. Finally, the media specialist places the order and sends all creative information needed to the selected Web sites. Once the order has been placed, the media specialist receives tracking and performance data and then compiles and analyzes the information in preparation for future ad campaigns.

REQUIREMENTS

High School

Although most media positions, including those at the entry level, require a bachelor's degree, you can prepare for a future job as media planner and/or buyer by taking specific courses offered at the high school level. These include advertising, business, cinematography, film and video, marketing, and radio and television. General liberal arts classes, such as communication, economics, English, and journalism, are also important, since media planners and buyers must be able to communicate clearly with both clients and coworkers. In addition, mathematics classes will give you the skills to work accurately with budget figures and placement costs.

Postsecondary Training

Increasingly, media planners and buyers have college degrees, often with majors in marketing or advertising. Even if you have prior work experience or training in media, you should select college classes that provide a good balance of business course work, broadcast and print experience, and liberal arts studies.

Business classes may include advertising, economics, marketing, and sales. Courses that focus on specific media, such as cinematography, film and video, radio and television, and new technologies (like the Internet), are also important. Additional classes in English, journalism, and speech will prove helpful as well. Media directors often need a master's degree, as well as extensive experience working with the various media.

Other Requirements

Media planners and buyers in broadcasting should have a keen understanding of programming and consumer buying trends, as well as a knowledge of each potential client's business. Print media specialists must be familiar with the process involved in creating print ads and the markets reached by various publications. In addition, all media workers need to be capable of maintaining good relationships with current clients, as well as pursuing new clients on a continual basis.

Communication and problem-solving skills are important, as are creativity, common sense, patience, and persistence. Media planners and buyers must also have excellent oral, written, and analytical skills; knowledge of interactive media planning trends and tools; and the ability to handle multiple assignments in a fast-paced work environment. Strategic thinking skills, industry interest, and computer experience with both database and word processing programs are also vital.

EXPLORING

Many high schools and two-year colleges and most four-year colleges have media departments that may include radio stations and public access or cable television channels. To gain worthwhile experience in media, you can work for these departments as aides, production assistants, programmers, or writers. In addition, high school and college newspapers and yearbooks often need students to sell advertising to local merchants. Theater departments frequently look for people to sell ads for performance programs.

In the local community, newspapers and other publications often hire high school students to work part time and/or in the summer in sales and clerical positions for the classified advertising department. Some towns have cable television stations that regularly look for volunteers to operate cameras, sell advertising, and coordinate various programs. In addition, a variety of religious-sponsored activities, such as craft fairs, holiday boutiques, and rummage sales, can pro-

Books to Read

Berkowitz, Ira. *Vault Career Guide to Advertising.* New York: Vault Inc., 2004.

Goodman, Jennifer. *Vault Career Guide to Marketing and Brand Management.* New York: Vault Inc., 2006.

Pattis, S. William. *Careers in Advertising.* 3d ed. New York: McGraw-Hill, 2004.

Steinberg, Margery. *Opportunities in Marketing Careers.* Rev. ed. New York: McGraw-Hill, 2005.

Vault Editors. *Vault Guide to the Top Advertising & Public Relations Employers.* New York: Vault Inc., 2008.

WetFeet. *Careers in Advertising and Public Relations.* San Francisco: WetFeet Inc., 2006.

vide you with opportunities to create and place ads and work with the local media to get exposure for the events.

EMPLOYERS

Media planners and buyers often work for advertising agencies in large cities, such as Chicago, Los Angeles, and New York. These agencies represent various clients that are trying to sell everything from financial services to dishwasher soap to the latest comedy featuring the hot star of the moment. Other media specialists work directly for radio and television networks, newspapers, magazines, and Web sites selling air time and print space. While many of these media organizations are located in large urban areas, particularly radio and television stations, most small towns put out newspapers and therefore need specialists to sell ad space and coordinate accounts. Approximately 51,000 advertising sales agents are employed in the advertising industry and related fields in the United States.

STARTING OUT

More than half of the jobs in print and broadcast media do not remain open long enough for companies to advertise available positions in the classified sections of newspapers. As a result, many media organizations, such as radio and television stations, do not usually advertise job openings in the want ads. Media planners and buyers often hear about available positions through friends, acquaintances, or family members and frequently enter the field as entry-level broadcasting or sales associates. Both broadcasting and sales can provide employees just starting out with experience in approaching and working for clients, as well as knowledge about the specifics of programming and its relation to selling air time.

Advertising agencies sometimes publicize job openings, both in local and national papers and on the Web. Competition is quite fierce for entry-level jobs, however, particularly at large agencies in big cities.

Print media employees often start working on smaller publications as in-house sales staff members, answering telephones and taking orders from customers. Other duties may include handling classified ads or coordinating the production and placement of small print ads created by in-house artists. While publications often advertise for entry-level positions, the best way to find work in advertising is to send resumes to as many agencies, publications, and broadcasting offices as possible. With any luck, your resume will arrive just as an opening is becoming available.

While you are enrolled in a college program, you should investigate opportunities for internships or on-campus employment in related areas. Your school's career planning center or placement office should have information on such positions. Previous experience often provides a competitive edge for all job seekers, but it is crucial to aspiring media planners and buyers.

ADVANCEMENT

Large agencies and networks often hire only experienced people, so it is common for media planners and buyers to learn the business at smaller companies. These opportunities allow media specialists to gain the experience and confidence they need to move up to more advanced positions. Jobs at smaller agencies and television and radio stations also provide possibilities for more rapid promotion than those at larger organizations.

Media planners and buyers climbing the company ladder can advance to the position of media director or may earn promotions to executive-level positions. For those already at the management level, advancement can come in the form of larger clients and more responsibility. In addition, many media planners and buyers who have experience with traditional media are investigating the opportunities and challenges that come with the job of interactive media planner/buyer or Web media specialist.

EARNINGS

Because media planners and buyers work for a variety of organizations all across the country and abroad, earnings can vary greatly. Media directors can earn between $46,000 and $130,000, depending on the type of employer and the director's experience level. For example, directors at small agencies make an average of $50,000, while those at large agencies can earn more than $120,000.

Media planners and buyers in television typically earn higher salaries than those in radio. In general, however, beginning broadcasting salespeople usually earn between $25,000 and $50,000 per year and can advance to as much as $35,000 after a few years of experience.

According to the U.S. Department of Labor, advertising sales agents earned salaries that ranged from less than $21,460 to more than $91,280 in 2006.

Most employers of media planners and buyers offer a variety of benefits, including health and life insurance, a retirement plan, and paid vacation and sick days.

WORK ENVIRONMENT

Although media planners and buyers often work a 40-hour week, their hours are not strictly nine to five. Sales calls, presentations, and meetings with ad space reps and clients are important parts of the job that usually have a profound effect on work schedules. In addition, media planners and buyers must invest considerable time investigating and reading about trends in programming, buying, and advertising.

The variety of opportunities for media planners and buyers results in a wide diversity of working conditions. Larger advertising agencies, publications, and networks may have modern and comfortable working facilities. Smaller markets may have more modest working environments.

Whatever the size of the organization, many planners seldom go into the office and must call in to keep in touch with the home organization. Travel is a big part of media planners' responsibilities to their clients, and they may have clients in many different types of businesses and services, as well as in different areas of the country.

While much of the media planner and buyer's job requires interaction with a variety of people, including coworkers, sales reps, supervisors, and clients, most media specialists also perform many tasks that require independent work, such as researching and writing reports. In any case, the media planner and buyer must be able to handle many tasks at the same time in a fast-paced, continually changing environment.

OUTLOOK

The employment outlook for media planners and buyers, like the outlook for the advertising industry itself, depends on the general health of the economy. When the economy thrives, companies produce an increasing number of goods and seek to promote them via newspapers, magazines, television, radio, the Internet, and various other media. The U.S. Department of Labor anticipates that employment in the advertising industry will grow 14 percent through 2016, faster than the average for all industries.

More and more people are relying on radio and television for their entertainment and information. With cable and local television channels offering a wide variety of programs, advertisers are increasingly turning to TV to get exposure for their products and services, as well as their public relations needs. Although newspaper sales are in decline, there is growth in special interest periodicals and other print publications. Interactive media, such as the Internet and CD catalogs, are providing a flurry of advertising activity all around the world. All of this activity will increase market opportunities for media planners and buyers.

Employment possibilities for media specialists are far greater in large cities, such as Chicago, Los Angeles, and New York, where most magazines and many broadcast networks are headquartered. However, smaller publications are often located in outlying areas, and large national organizations usually have sales offices in several cities across the country.

Competition for all advertising positions, including entry-level jobs, is expected to be intense. Media planners and buyers who have considerable experience will have the best chances of finding employment.

FOR MORE INFORMATION

For profiles of advertising workers and career information, contact
Advertising Educational Foundation
220 East 42nd Street, Suite 3300
New York, NY 10017-5806
Tel: 212-986-8060
http://www.aded.org

For information on college chapters, internship opportunities, and financial aid opportunities, contact
American Advertising Federation
1101 Vermont Avenue, NW, Suite 500
Washington, DC 20005-6306
Tel: 800-999-2231
Email: aaf@aaf.org
http://www.aaf.org

For information on advertising agencies, contact
American Association of Advertising Agencies
405 Lexington Avenue, 18th Floor
New York, NY 10174-1801
Tel: 212-682-2500
http://www.aaaa.org

For career resources and job listings, contact
American Marketing Association
311 South Wacker Drive, Suite 5800
Chicago, IL 60606-6629
Tel: 800-262-1150
http://www.marketingpower.com

For information on education and training, contact
Marketing Research Association
110 National Drive, 2nd Floor
Glastonbury, CT 06033-1212
Tel: 860-682-1000
Email: email@mra-net.org
http://www.mra-net.org

Media Relations
Specialists

QUICK FACTS

School Subjects
Business
English
Speech

Personal Skills
Communication/ideas
Leadership/management

Work Environment
Primarily indoors
Primarily one location

Minimum Education Level
Bachelor's degree

Salary Range
$28,080 to $60,330 to
$89,220+

Certification or Licensing
Voluntary

Outlook
Much faster than the average

DOT
165

GOE
01.03.01

NOC
0611

O*NET-SOC
27-3031.00

OVERVIEW

Media relations specialists are experienced *public relations specialists* who have a broad working knowledge of television, radio, and print journalism and skills in establishing a controlled, positive image in the media for a company, person, or organization. Also referred to as *communications consultants,* media relations specialists serve as the liaison between the company, person, or organization they represent and newspaper, magazine, and broadcast news editors and reporters. The number of people working in media relations and their locations falls within the same parameters as public relations specialists. There are approximately 29,000 public relations specialists employed in advertising and related industries in the United States.

HISTORY

Similar to public relations, media relations is rooted in the 19th century, when newspapers began running positive articles about businesses that advertised in the paper to encourage future advertising. By the early 20th century, literary bureaus were established to contrive these articles, and publicity agents began surfacing in large cities. However, the articles began to undermine the newspapers' objectivity, and the practice was soon halted in the United States.

But the link between media relations and newspapers endured through reporters who were willing to use language's effects on public image to present a company or organization in a positive light. By the end of World War II, government agencies and politicians followed business's example by hiring public relations specialists to help deliver information to the press and to advise them on their appearances at press conferences and interviews.

Media relations is now an essential function of public relations. Virtually every public relations agency either employs media relations specialists or assigns media relations duties for each client to account executives. Likewise, most large companies and organizations have someone in charge of media relations.

THE JOB

As Wendy Leinhart, media specialist with Marcy Monyak & Associates in Chicago, emphasizes, "Media relations is not a stand-alone job; it is a function of public relations." In other words, media relations is just one, but perhaps the most significant, part of public relations.

Media relations specialists develop corporate or product positioning strategies for specific media outlets; plan photo and editorial opportunities for use in the media and develop editorial ideas to fit a publication's or broadcast medium's special promotions; develop news and feature releases and pitch them to the media; place articles with the media; gain favorable product reviews and publicize them to the media; position the organization they represent as an expert source; execute media events, such as press conferences, interviews, tours, and promotions; handle information requests from the press; and collect and analyze media coverage of the organization they represent.

To understand the media relations specialist's work, suppose a large pharmaceutical company has to recall one of its products because of possible tampering. The company's CEO decides she wants to address the issue with the public. The media relations specialist decides between arranging a press conference or an interview with a newspaper journalist from a major newspaper, contacts the appropriate media (in the case of a press conference) or reporter (in the case of an interview), and then briefs the CEO as to the angles on which the reporter or reporters will be basing questions.

Successful media relations depends on building an authentic rapport with reporters and editors while giving them something they can use. Media relations specialists are aware that most reliable journalists despise news that originates with a public relations slant, but that journalists often must rely on it because of time constraints. This is the reason rapport-building skills are essential in media relations.

Because the press release is at the heart of media relations, and major newspapers and wire services receive thousands of releases each day, the experienced media relations specialist knows when something is actually newsworthy and presents it in the most concise, attractive, and easy-to-read manner as possible.

REQUIREMENTS

High School

While your overall schedule should be college preparatory, there are a number of classes you should emphasize during your high school career. Naturally, English and communication classes, such as speech or debate, should be a top priority as they will help you hone your communication skills. Also, take computer classes and other courses that emphasize working with different media, such as radio or television broadcasting and journalism. Courses in business, economics, and mathematics will help you develop the skills you will need to work with budgets and project planning. If your high school offers advertising or marketing classes, be sure to take those. Finally, since a media relations specialist is involved with current events, take any history or social studies class that emphasizes this subject. Such a class will give you the opportunity to observe how current events are related to the public through different media and the influences these media can have.

Postsecondary Training

To become a media relations specialist, you should have at least a bachelor's degree in communications, public relations, or journalism. Many college programs require or encourage their students to complete internships in public relations, either during the school year or the summer. These internships often provide valuable hands-on experience. Typical classes for those majoring in public relations include public relations management; writing courses that cover news releases, speeches, and proposals; and visual communications such as computer graphics. Other courses you should take include psychology, sociology, and business administration. A master's degree may be helpful as you advance in your career.

Certification or Licensing

Although certification or licensing are not required, you may find it beneficial to get accreditation in the communications field. The

Public Relations Society of America accredits public relations professionals of at least five years' experience with the *accredited in public relations* designation, which can be obtained by passing a written and oral examination. The International Association of Business Communicators also offers the accredited business communicator designation.

Other Requirements
In addition to excellent verbal and written communication skills, you need to be creative and aggressive, coming up with new and appealing ideas to attract media interest in your clients. You also must be able to work under the pressure of deadlines, make decisions quickly and effectively, and do thorough research. As a media relations specialist, you should have an interest in continuously learning about new technologies and using these new technologies to promote the interests of your clients.

EXPLORING

During your high school years, become involved with the school newspaper, yearbook, or literary magazine. Try working with these publications' advertising departments or sections, either selling ad space or promoting the publication to the student body. You can also join school committees that plan and publicize events such as school dances, fundraisers, or other functions. Try your hand at other media by working at the school television or radio station. You may even be able to come up with your own ad campaign for a school event.

The best way to explore this career during your college years is to complete an internship at a public relations firm. Try getting a part-time or summer job at a local newspaper, radio, or television station where you can work in some type of public relations department. Read publications by the Public Relations Society of America (http://www.prsa.org/publications), such as *The Strategist* and *Public Relations Tactics,* to become more familiar with how the public relations field works.

EMPLOYERS

Media relations specialists are employed either by the organization, company, or individual they represent or by a public relations agency. While the majority of opportunities are in large metropolitan areas, prospects may exist even in smaller communities, such as at colleges and universities. The number of people working in media relations and their locations falls within the same parameters as public relations specialists. Approximately 29,000 public relations specialists are employed in advertising and related industries in the United States.

STARTING OUT

It is not likely that you'll begin your career in media relations right after graduating from college. Even someone with a professional journalism background should not jump into media relations without first working as a public relations generalist. "Most media relations specialists work entry-level PR jobs after working as a journalist, and fall into media relations as a specialty," Wendy Leinhart says. Also important is computer literacy, as the proliferation of online services continues.

College career services counselors can help you find a position that will prepare you for media relations. Other effective routes include completing an internship at a public relations agency or in a corporate public relations or communications department.

ADVANCEMENT

Entry-level public relations specialists might assemble media clippings or create media lists for different clients. As they gain experience, they may be assigned to write news releases, conduct a poll or survey, or write speeches for company officials.

As prospective media relations specialists become more experienced and knowledgeable about the organization they represent, they may help seasoned media relations specialists pitch news releases, place articles with the media, and plan media events.

Seasoned media relations specialists can move into managerial positions where they take an active role in shaping media strategies and positioning the organization they represent.

EARNINGS

Salaried public relations specialists employed in advertising and related industries earned mean salaries of $60,330 in 2006, according to the U.S. Department of Labor. Salaries for all public relations specialists ranged from less than $28,080 to $89,220 or more.

Media relations specialists working for consulting firms, agencies, and large corporations earn the most, while those in the nonprofit sector earn less.

Media relations specialists receive standard benefits, including health insurance, paid vacations, and sick days. They also receive regular salary increases and are often given expense accounts.

WORK ENVIRONMENT

Media relations specialists usually work in a traditional office environment and work between 40 and 50 hours per week. From time to time, tight project deadlines may call for more overtime than usual. Media relations specialists are expected to be tastefully dressed and socially poised and to maintain a professional demeanor. Often, they must entertain editors and reporters at lunches or dinners. Frequently, their conduct in their personal life is important if they are employed by a public relations agency or as a consultant to a client. Media relations specialists also are required to travel from time to time for business.

OUTLOOK

Competition among corporations continues to grow, as does the competition between nonprofit organizations for funding. In addition, individuals in the public eye, such as politicians and sports figures, continue to want expert advice on shaping their images. Thus, public relations will remain among the fastest-growing fields, and media relations as a component of public relations will continue to grow. The U.S. Department of Labor predicts that employment for public relations specialists employed in advertising and related industries will grow much faster than the average for all occupations through 2016.

Competition for media relations positions will be stiff because, as with public relations, so many job seekers are enticed by the perceived glamour and appeal of the field. However, those with journalism backgrounds will have an advantage.

FOR MORE INFORMATION

For information on certification and Communications World *magazine, contact*

International Association of Business Communicators
One Halladie Plaza, Suite 600
San Francisco, CA 94102-2842
Tel: 415-544-4700
Email: service centre@iabc.com
http://www.iabc.com

For career, certification, and student membership information, contact
Public Relations Society of America
Career Information
33 Maiden Lane, 11th Floor
New York, NY 10038-5150
Tel: 212-460-1400
Email: prssa@prsa.org (student membership)
http://www.prsa.org

For information on program accreditation and professional development, contact
Canadian Public Relations Society
4195 Dundas Street West, Suite 346
Toronto, ON M8X 1Y4 Canada
Tel: 416-239-7034
Email: admin@cprs.ca
http://www.cprs.ca

Merchandise Displayers

OVERVIEW

Merchandise displayers, sometimes known as *visual merchandisers*, design and install displays of clothing, accessories, furniture, and other products to attract customers. They set up displays in windows and showcases and on the sales floors of retail stores. Display workers who specialize in dressing mannequins are known as *model dressers*. Those who specialize in installing displays in store windows are known as *window dressers* or *window trimmers*. These workers use their artistic flair and imagination to create excitement and customer interest in the store. They also work with other types of merchandise to develop exciting images, product campaigns, and shopping concepts. There are approximately 87,000 merchandise displayers and window trimmers employed in the United States.

HISTORY

Eye-catching displays of merchandise attract customers and encourage them to buy. This form of advertising has been used throughout history. In the past, farmers who displayed their produce at markets were careful to place their largest, most tempting fruits and vegetables at the top of the baskets. Peddlers opened their bags and cases and arranged their wares in attractive patterns. Store owners decorated their windows with collections of articles they hoped to sell. Their business success often was a matter of chance, however, and depended heavily on their own persuasiveness and sales ability.

As glass windows became less expensive, storefronts were able to accommodate larger window frames. This exposed more of the store to passersby, and stores soon found that decorative window displays were effective in attracting customers. Today, a customer may see nearly the entire store and the displays of the products it sells just by looking in the front window.

The advent of self-service stores has minimized the importance of the salesperson's personal touch. The merchandise now has to sell itself. Displays have become an important inducement for customers to buy. Advertising will bring people into stores, but an appealing product display can make the difference between a customer who merely browses and one who buys.

Merchandise displayers are needed year-round, but during the Christmas season they often execute their most elaborate work. Small retail stores generally depend on the owner or manager to create the merchandise displays, or they may hire a freelance window dresser on a part-time basis. Large retail operations, such as department stores, retain a permanent staff of display and visual merchandising specialists. Competition among these stores is intense, and their success depends on capturing a significant portion of the market. Therefore, they allocate a large share of their publicity budget to creating unique, captivating displays.

THE JOB

Using their imagination and creative ability, as well as their knowledge of color harmony, composition, and other fundamentals of art and interior design, merchandise displayers in retail establishments create an idea for a setting designed to show off merchandise and attract customers' attention. Often the display is planned around a theme or concept. After the display manager approves the design or idea, the display workers create the display. They install background settings, such as carpeting, wallpaper, and lighting, gather props and other accessories, arrange mannequins and merchandise, and place price tags and descriptive signs where they are needed.

Displayers may be assisted by carpenters, painters, or store maintenance workers. Displayers may use merchandise from various departments of the store or props from previous displays. Sometimes they borrow special items that their business doesn't carry from other stores; for example, toys or sports equipment. The displays are dismantled and new ones installed every few weeks. In very large stores that employ many display workers, displayers may specialize in carpentry, painting, making signs, or setting up interior or window displays. A *display director* usually supervises and coordinates the display workers' activities and confers with other managers to select merchandise to be featured.

Ambitious and talented display workers have many possible career avenues. The importance of visual merchandising is being recognized more and more as retail establishments compete for consumer dollars. Some display workers can advance to display director or even a position in store planning.

In addition to traditional stores, the skills of *visual marketing workers* are now in demand in many other types of establishments. Restaurants often try to present a distinct image to enhance the dining experience. Outlet stores, discount malls, and entertainment centers also use visual marketing to establish their identities with the public. Chain stores often need to make changes in or redesign all their stores and turn to display professionals for their expertise. Consumer product manufacturers also are heavily involved in visual marketing. They hire display and design workers to create exciting concepts, such as in-store shops, that present a unified image of the manufacturer's products and are sold as complete units to retail stores.

Opportunities for employment also exist with store fixture manufacturers. Many companies build and sell specialized props, banners, signs, displays, and mannequins and hire display workers as sales representatives to promote their products. The display workers' understanding of retail needs and their insight into the visual merchandising industry make them valuable consultants.

This occupation appeals to imaginative, artistic individuals who find it rewarding to use their creative abilities to visualize a design concept and transform it into reality. Original, creative displays grow out of an awareness of current design trends and popular themes. Although display workers use inanimate objects such as props and materials, an understanding of human motivations helps them create displays with strong customer appeal.

REQUIREMENTS

High School

To work as a display worker, you must have at least a high school diploma. Important high school subjects include art, mechanical drawing, merchandising, and woodworking.

Postsecondary Training

Some employers require college courses in advertising, art, fashion design, interior decorating, or related subjects. Community and junior colleges that offer advertising and marketing courses may include display work in the curriculum. Fashion merchandising schools and fine arts institutes also offer courses useful to display workers.

Much of the training for display workers is gained on the job. They generally start as helpers for routine tasks, such as carrying props and dismantling sets. Gradually they are permitted to build simple props and work up to constructing more difficult displays. As they become more experienced, display workers who show artistic talent may be assigned to plan simple designs. The total training time varies depending on the beginner's ability and the variety and complexity of the displays.

Other Requirements
Besides education and experience, you will also need creative ability, manual dexterity, and mechanical aptitude to do this work. You should possess the strength and physical stamina needed to carry equipment and climb ladders. You also need agility to work in close quarters without upsetting the props.

EXPLORING

To explore the work of merchandise displayers, try to get a part-time or summer job with a department or retail store or at a convention center. This will give you an overview of the display operations in these establishments. Photographers and theater groups need helpers to work with props and sets, although some may require previous experience or knowledge related to their work. Your school's drama and photo clubs may offer opportunities to learn basic design concepts. You also should read about this line of work; *Display & Design Ideas* (http://www.ddimagazine.com) publishes articles on the field and related subjects.

EMPLOYERS

Approximately 87,000 merchandise displayers and window trimmers are employed in the United States. Most work in department and clothing stores, but many are employed in other types of retail stores, such as variety, drug, and shoe stores. Some have their own design businesses, and some are employed by design firms that handle interior and professional window dressing for small stores. Employment of display workers is distributed throughout the country, with most of the jobs concentrated in large towns and cities.

Did You Know?

- There are approximately 48,000 advertising and public relations firms in the United States.
- About 505,000 people are employed in the advertising and public relations industries.
- Approximately 74 percent of advertising workers are between the ages of 25 and 54.
- Advertising industry professionals work an average of 34.7 hours per week—slightly higher than the average for all occupations.
- More than 20 percent of advertising workers are employed in California and New York.
- Employment in advertising and public relations is expected to grow by 14 percent through 2016—or faster than the average for all industries.

Source: U.S. Department of Labor

STARTING OUT

School career services offices may have job listings for display workers or related positions. Individuals wishing to become display workers can apply directly to retail stores, decorating firms, or exhibition centers. Openings also may be listed in the classified ads of newspapers.

Some experienced merchandise displayers choose to work as freelance designers. Competition in this area, however, is intense, and it takes time to establish a reputation, build a list of clients, and earn an adequate income. Freelancing part time while holding down another job provides a more secure income for many display workers. Freelancing also provides beginners with opportunities to develop a portfolio of photographs of their best designs, which they can then use to sell their services to other stores.

ADVANCEMENT

Display workers with supervisory ability can become regional managers. Further advancement may lead to a position as a display director or head of store planning.

Another way to advance is by starting a freelance design business. This can be done with very little financial investment, although freelance design workers must spend many long hours generating new business and establishing a reputation in the field.

Experienced display workers also may be able to transfer their skills to jobs in other art-related fields, such as interior design or photography. This move, however, requires additional training.

EARNINGS

According to the U.S. Department of Labor, the median annual earnings of merchandise displayers were $23,820 in 2006. The lowest 10 percent earned less than $15,630 and the highest 10 percent earned more than $41,370. Displayers employed in clothing stores earned a mean salary of $32,280 in 2006.

Freelance displayers may earn more than $35,000 a year, but their income depends entirely on their talent, reputation, number of clients, and amount of time they work.

WORK ENVIRONMENT

Display workers usually work 35 to 40 hours a week, except during busy seasons, such as Christmas. Selling promotions and increased sales drives during targeted seasons can require the display staff to work extra hours in the evenings and on weekends.

Constructing and installing displays requires prolonged standing, bending, stooping, and working in awkward positions. There is some risk of falling off ladders or being injured from handling sharp materials or tools, but serious injuries are uncommon.

OUTLOOK

Employment for display workers is expected to grow about as fast as the average for all occupations through 2016, according to the U.S. Department of Labor. Growth in this profession is expected due to an expanding retail sector and the increasing popularity of visual merchandising. Most openings will occur as older, experienced workers retire or leave the occupation.

Fluctuations in our nation's economy affect the volume of retail sales because people are less likely to spend money during recessionary times. For display workers this can result in layoffs or hiring freezes.

FOR MORE INFORMATION

For information on student membership, scholarship opportunities, schools with student chapters, and additional career materials, contact

American Society of Interior Designers
608 Massachusetts Avenue, NE
Washington, DC 20002-6006
Tel: 202-546-3480
http://www.asid.org

For membership information, contact

Institute of Store Planners
25 North Broadway
Tarrytown, NY 10590-3221
Tel: 914-332-0040
Email: info@ispo.org
http://www.ispo.org

To read about industry events and news, check out the following magazine's Web site:

Display & Design Ideas
http://www.ddimagazine.com

Models

QUICK FACTS

School Subjects
Art
Theater/dance

Personal Skills
Artistic
Following instructions

Work Environment
Indoors and outdoors
Primarily multiple locations

Minimum Education Level
High school diploma

Salary Range
$15,000 to $23,000 to
$1 million+

Certification or Licensing
None available

Outlook
About as fast as the average

DOT
297

GOE
01.09.01

NOC
5232

O*NET-SOC
41-9011.00, 41-9012.00

OVERVIEW

Models display a wide variety of products and services in print, such as magazines and newspapers, on television, and in live marketing. *Industrial models* are used in all advertising media to sell every kind of product or service imaginable. *Fashion models* display clothing and fashion accessories in fashion shows, apparel catalogs, and retail stores. A small segment of the modeling field is devoted to posing for commercial and fine artists.

Approximately 17,000 demonstrators and product promoters (including models) are employed in advertising and related industries.

HISTORY

As long as there have been artists, there have been models who posed for them. In earlier times, many of these models were the friends or relatives of the artist. Wealthy patrons also posed for artists to have their portraits painted. Actresses, actors, society personalities, and other celebrities were among the first models.

In 1858, Charles Frederick Worth, an English tailor, opened a salon, or fashion house, in Paris and became the first dressmaker to display his designs on live models.

The history of the photographic model is comparatively recent. Although the modern camera was invented by George Eastman in 1889, its possible uses in commercial advertising were not realized for more than 20 years. Shortly after the turn of the century, when the ready-to-wear clothing industry began to grow rapidly, businesses discovered that a picture could sell more products than text, and fashion professionals realized that live models boosted clothing sales more than mannequins. Consequently, advertisements began to feature pictures of young women who seemed to endorse a manufacturer's product. As commercial photography continued to grow and develop, so did the career of the photographic model. Today these models can be male or female, and of every age, race, and color, depending on the advertiser's target market.

The story of fashion models begins in Paris, where they were first employed more than a century ago to display the exclusive clothing designed by French dressmakers for wealthy women. Before 1900, U.S. fashions were, for the most part, copies of the French originals, and it was seldom considered necessary for copied clothing to be shown by live models. Shortly after World War I, the U.S. garment industry created some original designs. These garments were mass produced. As these fashion houses slowly multiplied, so did the number of models needed to present new clothing designs to prospective buyers. In the past 40 years, the U.S. garment industry has assumed world leadership in the production of clothing, and increasing numbers of models have been needed to display these garments and the fashion accessories that go with them.

THE JOB

Models generally are grouped according to the medium or media in which they work. For instance, models who perform with movement in fashion shows and for retail stores (on the floor) are known as fashion models. Those who pose for artists are known as *artists' models,* and those who advertise products and services in print are known as *photographic models.* In large cities, modeling agencies specialize in handling petite, plus-size, specialty, character, beauty, photographic, and high fashion models.

Artists' models pose for an individual artist or for a class of art students. When posing, models must stand or sit in one position for several hours at a time. A quick break for relaxation is usually given once each hour. Often the model must pose on a platform under hot and bright lights and sometimes wear little or no clothing. One job may last a day, while another may last for several weeks.

Photographic models pose for photographs. Their job is to lend attractiveness to an advertisement and enhance the desirability of the product. These models encounter a great variety of situations in their work. One series of photographs may be taken in a studio under hot lights with the model wearing a heavy fur coat. Another may be taken outdoors in midwinter with the model wearing only a bathing suit. One job may last only an hour, while another may require an entire day. Models may travel to other states or even to other countries to be photographed in beautiful, unusual, or exotic settings.

Rarely do photographic models work full time. Days or weeks may pass between one job and the next, especially if they work on a freelance basis. If models contract with a modeling agency, however, their schedule may be fuller because the agency will secure modeling assignments for them.

The photographic model who has some acting ability may land a job in a television commercial. These ads are usually videotaped or filmed. Although television modeling is very lucrative, it is difficult for the average model to break into this field, mainly due to lack of training in acting.

Specialty models must possess particular features that are photogenic, such as hands, feet, legs, hair, lips, or ears that will help sell specific products.

Fashion models differ from the other types of models in three basic ways. First, the models usually work for clothing manufacturers, fashion designers, or department stores on a full-time basis. Second, they do not merely pose in one position, but walk around and assume a variety of poses in their display of the clothing. Third, they often speak to prospective purchasers to inform them of the model number and price of each garment.

Some fashion models may be employed by clothing manufacturers as showroom and fitting models. In many large department stores, a staff of full-time models (called *floor models*) is employed to promote the sale of various garments or accessories. The store may have a regularly scheduled style show during the daily lunch hour; at other times, models may walk throughout the store showing apparel and talking with customers about the garments and accessories being worn. Models hired by a distributor to hand out free product samples, such as perfume or food, are known as *sampling demonstration models* or *product promoters.*

All fashion models employ certain techniques to display their clothing in the most effective way. Immaculate grooming is basic for most models, from the proper application of makeup and hair care to the smallest personal details. Models must walk gracefully with an erect carriage and master the techniques of pivoting to show the sides and back of a garment. They must know how to carry their hands and arms gracefully, as well as the body positions needed to emphasize certain details of their costume. They also must be able to call attention to accessories, such as purses, jewelry, and gloves.

Some fashion models do not work regularly but are called only for special style shows or certain buyers' showings. Some prefer to

A model displays the latest fashion for buyers and other industry professionals during Fashion Week. *(Dima Gavrysh, AP Images)*

freelance since they may have other jobs or responsibilities. The most successful models work in all areas of the field, from live fashion modeling to print work to video and film modeling, as well as acting and live industrial and promotional presentations.

REQUIREMENTS

High School

There are no standard educational requirements for models. Most employers of photographic models prefer at least a high school education. Courses such as home economics, photography, and sewing are helpful. Classes in dance, fencing, Asian arts such as Tai Chi, and other studies that focus on body and movement control provide a good foundation for modeling. Public speaking and business courses are helpful since models often work as freelancers.

Postsecondary Training

Many employers of models state a preference for college graduates with the ability to communicate well and with a general cultural background. Academic courses may include art, art history, debate, drama, English, history, photography, or speech. Some models take special courses in sports or physical fitness, such as aerobics, dance, horseback riding, skating, skiing, or swimming to get into and stay in shape and develop physical coordination, suppleness, and grace. As models often keep track of their own expenses, a basic knowledge of bookkeeping and mathematics is helpful.

Other Requirements

There are significant differences in the requirements necessary for each type of model. The major requirement for the fashion model is, of course, physical appearance. Although most people think of all models as being young and slender, that is not necessarily the case. No set standard exists for a model's physical description because many different body types are needed. Many garment manufacturers seek female fashion models who are between the ages of 16 and 30, between 5 feet 8 inches and 5 feet 11 inches in height and wear from a size six to a size 10. Male models generally must be between 6 feet and 6 feet 2 inches in height and wear a size 40 or 42 regular suit. People who fail to meet these specifications, however, should realize that possibilities may still exist for them in this career—after all, garments and other fashion items are made for people of all sizes and types. Also, atypical models who do not necessarily possess classical model features, proportions, or body types, but display interesting or unusual personal style, increasingly are being seen on runways and in photo advertisements, reflecting designer, commercial, and public acceptance of cultural and physical diversity and individual expression in fashion.

Because some fashion houses create styles for people of middle years whose weight is closer to average, more mature-looking models sometimes are needed. Other firms that specialize in evening clothes often require models of above average height to display their garments. Companies that produce junior sizes require models who can wear those sizes without alterations. Manufacturers of misses' or women's sizes may seek models who can wear size eight, 10, or 12. They also may seek full-figured models who wear size 14 or larger. Petite models are 5 feet 5 inches and wear uneven sizes such as three, five, and seven.

The basic requirement for photographers' models is that they photograph well. It must be emphasized, however, that not all attractive people have the qualities that commercial photographers require. Many times characteristics such as wholesomeness and sincerity, as well as freshness of face or manner, are as important in this field as good looks.

Modeling is a particularly fatiguing occupation because it requires many hours of standing and walking, or sitting or standing still in uncomfortable positions. Thus, good health and physical stamina are important. In addition, those interested in being fashion or photographic models must be prepared to give up most of their social life and limit their diets. To maintain their figures and appearances, they will require many extra hours of sleep each night and will need to avoid rich foods and beverages.

Another important requirement is immaculate grooming. Fashion and photographic models spend more hours than the average person taking care of their skin, hair, nails, and general physical fitness. Especially important to fashion models is the ability to walk gracefully while carrying their hands, arms, and torso in a poised and chic manner.

Most fashion and photographers' models must have special training to meet all of the above requirements. Entering a reputable modeling school to learn the skills and techniques of modeling or enrolling in a good charm school to learn makeup application, appropriate clothing, and the proper ways to walk and stand are also helpful and can be a shortcut into the business.

EXPLORING

If you are an aspiring model, you should read about the modeling industry and contact modeling agencies to gain an understanding of what their needs may include. Experience in fashion modeling may be obtained in home economics courses as well as from local fashion shows. Many fashion design schools stage shows for their students' designs and need amateur models to donate their time.

You may want to talk with the buyer or fashion director of a large local store or seek the advice of a commercial photographer (who often help new talent get started) about your opportunities for a successful modeling career and the special areas for which you may be qualified. Modeling agencies also may be approached for their opinions. It is important to assess your chances for meaningful work before moving to a big city or investing in expensive modeling classes, photographs, and wardrobe.

EMPLOYERS

Approximately 17,000 demonstrators and product promoters (including models) are employed in advertising and related industries. Models work in a variety of settings that require different skills and qualifications. Fashion models may be employed by apparel firms or retail stores; photographic models work through one or more agencies for a variety of clients. High fashion models usually work in major fashion centers such as London, New York, or Paris.

Large cities generally offer more opportunities for modeling work than small towns.

A large percentage of those in the modeling industry do not work full time as models, since there are far more applicants than assignments. Therefore many models have other means of supporting themselves. Models generally choose part-time jobs, especially those with flexible schedules or evening work, to be available for auditions and assignments. Many work as restaurant servers, though individuals with special skills or training may find other work. Some work in sales, which allows them flexibility in schedules and number of hours.

STARTING OUT

To gain employment as an artist's model, men or women may apply directly to various art schools or the state employment office. Cautiously check newspaper want ads.

Graduates of modeling schools may be aided by school career services offices in securing their first job. Another possibility for the prospective model is to register at a modeling agency. Aspiring models, however, should be wary of disreputable agencies or schools that promise jobs for a fee toward the purchase of a portfolio of photographs or a contract for modeling classes. Legitimate agencies and modeling schools are listed in industry publications. Choose a modeling agency certified by such organizations as the Screen Actors Guild (SAG) or check with your local Better Business Bureau or Chamber of Commerce to make sure the agency or school is licensed by the state education department before signing an agreement or paying money to an agency or service that promises jobs.

Many agencies select only those people with qualities they feel will be demanded by their clients. If accepted by an agency, the future model's composite card and photographs are placed on file and the model will be called when the agency has a job for which the person is qualified. In return for the agency's services, models pay 15 to 20 percent of their earnings to the agency.

All models who wish to have a career in modeling are required to have a collection of photographs to show prospective employers. These photographs should include at least one head shot and several full-length shots in various kinds of situations and garments to show the model's versatility and ability to sell whatever he or she is modeling. Photographic models must have multiple copies of these photographs to leave with potential employers. The back of each picture should list the model's name, address, a contact phone number, height, weight, and coloring, along with clothing and shoe sizes. This picture will be placed in a file along with pictures of many other models. When someone of this type and size is needed for a picture, the model may be called to pose. Models include tear sheets in their portfolios from the assignments they have completed. These sheets prove to prospective employers the model's experience and ability.

Aspiring models who seek work in a large, unfamiliar city should go there prepared to look for a job for at least three months. They should have enough money to support themselves and pay for such modeling necessities as a fashionable wardrobe, professional hair and beauty care, adequate diet, and such incidentals as additional photographs or special short-term training.

ADVANCEMENT

For artists' models, advancement may take the form of higher hourly wages modeling at the better art schools and for the more successful artists. Advancement for fashion or photographic models means increased income and greater demand for their talent. However, their careers usually are short. The model who works in the field for longer than eight years is considered highly unusual. Certain physical changes and lifestyles often make it difficult for older people to compete with younger models for the same type of assignments.

Even a high degree of success can lead to the shortening of a model's career. When models appear too frequently on magazine covers or in features, the uniqueness of their look becomes familiar, and they are passed over in favor of models who have not received such wide coverage. Also, models who become identified with one particular product, such as a line of makeup or shampoo, may find it difficult to qualify for jobs with other employers.

Most fashion and photographic models must learn a marketable skill or profession to which they may turn when they can no longer continue modeling. Many fashion models gain enough knowledge to move into advertising, fashion design, public relations, or retailing. Others attend special schools between modeling assignments to learn business, technical, or vocational skills. Still others go to work for modeling agencies or open agencies of their own. Modeling can be a gateway to consulting jobs in the fashion and merchandising field, and some models serve as board members of fashion magazines. Other models become actors and actresses. Well-known models may develop their own line of cosmetics or other products.

EARNINGS

Earnings for models vary according to experience and depend on the number, length, and type of assignments he or she receives. Today, top fashion models working full time for wholesalers or retailers earn approximately $40,000 or more a year. Models working retail shows earn between $15,000 and $18,000 or more each year. Female models working for agencies make $100 to $125 an hour. Hourly wages are higher for photographic models working in large metropolitan cities such as Chicago, Los Angeles, Miami, or New York, and for models who are in great demand. Top photographic models signed to exclusive contracts with cosmetic firms may earn $1 million or more per year. Almost all models work with agents and pay 15 to 20 percent of their earnings in return for an agent's services.

The U.S. Department of Labor reports that models earned median salaries of $23,340 in 2006. The lowest 10 percent earned less than $15,960, and the highest 10 percent earned more than $38,850.

Demonstrators and product promoters earned salaries that ranged from less than $16,020 to $40,090 or more in 2006, with a median salary of $22,150.

Models who appear in television commercials are paid according to fee schedules set up by the two major unions, the Screen Actors Guild (SAG) and the American Federation of Television and Radio Artists (AFTRA). Models who speak earn more than those who do not. In addition, they receive residual fee whenever the commercial is aired.

Floor models employed by department stores earn the same salary as salespeople. The rate of pay is generally between $8 and $12 an hour, depending on the size and location of the store and the quality and cost of the merchandise. Models who work for advertising agencies may earn between $15 and $25 an hour. The more versatile the model, the greater the opportunity for employment.

Because they are seldom employed full time, instead earning a high hourly fee on an occasional basis, photographic models may not always have enough money to maintain themselves between jobs. They may find it necessary to seek other kinds of work on a temporary basis. Since it is essential that they have outstanding wardrobes, they frequently work at part-time jobs to buy the necessary clothes for their assignments. Models occasionally receive clothing or clothing discounts instead of, or in addition to, regular earnings.

The only full-time employment for models usually is as a spokesperson for a store or company. Full-time models usually receive up to two or three weeks of vacation per year. The perks of being a fashion model include the chance to wear beautiful clothes, look your best, and be groomed by photographers, designers, artists, and hair and makeup professionals. Some models travel to exciting places and meet interesting and famous people; a very few may even attain celebrity status. Indeed, today's fashion and cosmetics supermodels have achieved a celebrity status that formerly was the exclusive domain of movie stars.

Historically, the industry favors youth, but older models are being used by agencies more often and the age barrier seems to be coming down. Young people who hope to become models, however, should approach the career with the understanding that competition is keen and that it may take years of work to attain success. But even the beginner, on a local level, can make enough money to make this career worthwhile.

WORK ENVIRONMENT

Modeling can be exciting, challenging, glamorous, and rewarding, but also very stressful. Modeling is not a routine job and to be successful, models must have the drive, patience, and self-confidence to adjust and meet new challenges. They also must be able to accept rejection, since many assignments require auditions where many qualified applicants compete.

Models work under a variety of conditions. The artist's model usually works indoors in a loft, a studio, or a classroom. These rooms may be large and drafty with high ceilings and inadequate heating or cooling facilities. The more modern art schools, however, will be comfortably heated, ventilated, and lighted. This model may pose in ordinary street clothing, in exotic costumes, or in body-revealing attire.

Photographic models may work either indoors or outdoors. There may be times when models are asked to pose in bathing suits while standing outside in chilly weather. At other times, they may model wool clothing in midsummer on hot city pavements. In photographers' studios, models often are asked to hold a pose for a long period of time while lights and background details are adjusted. Models need patience to wait while problems are solved and many different people offer opinions about any one shot.

Many agency models must carry heavy bags of cosmetics, grooming tools, accessories, and garments as they travel from one client to another.

Fashion models usually work indoors in comfortable show-rooms, hotels, or restaurants. They must stand and walk a great deal during busy seasons. During slack seasons, runway and show-room models may have little to do and time may pass slowly. If they are employed in a department store, models are able to walk about the store and talk with customers. Although they are on their feet for most of the working day, they enjoy a variety of settings and people in their work.

Models must like their work thoroughly and not allow themselves to become impatient or exasperated by rejection, delays, or disappointments. Many young persons who enter a modeling career do so because they anticipate that it will be glamorous. Once embarked upon the career, they find little glamour and much hard work. Nevertheless, there are many satisfactions to be found in achieving success in this demanding field. Most models enjoy dressing well and looking trim and fit. They enjoy the excitement of the fashion and advertising worlds. They may find that the people with whom they work are interesting and may have an opportunity to meet or to work with famous or successful persons. Although their careers as models may be short, often they have a worthwhile second career in advertising, business, fashion, or public relations.

OUTLOOK

The U.S. Department of Labor (USDL) predicts employment for models to grow about as fast as the average for all occupations through 2016, but job competition will be fierce because this career attracts so many people. The number of fashion models seeking jobs is far greater than the number of openings. Many jobs exist for artists' models, but their income almost never is enough to live on. Part-time work is easier to find than full-time work. The number of models working should increase as the economy becomes more global. Models from the United States are in demand around the world. Opportunities for male models should also increase as the public becomes more open to the marketing of men's fashions. Most openings will occur as models quit or retire to pursue other employment or interests.

Opportunities for demonstrators and product promoters (including those employed in advertising and related industries) should be better. The USDL predicts that employment for these workers will grow by 18 percent—or faster than the average—through 2016. Their services will be increasingly needed at trade shows and for in-store promotions at retail shops.

FOR MORE INFORMATION

Aspiring models should gather information from a variety of sources: agencies, books, and articles. Little information is available to help students in their choices other than checking schools and agencies with the local Better Business Bureau or Chamber of Commerce and talking with experienced models. The SAG and the AFTRA do not represent models unless they become actors.

For information on modeling careers and annual conventions, visit
International Modeling and Talent Association
http://www.imta.com

To read about fashions, models, and agencies, visit
Models.com
http://models.com

Photo Stylists

QUICK FACTS

School Subjects
Art
Business

Personal Skills
Artistic
Communication/ideas

Work Environment
Indoors and outdoors
Primarily multiple locations

Minimum Education Level
Some postsecondary training

Salary Range
$150 to $350 to $500+
per day

Certification or Licensing
None available

Outlook
About as fast as the average

DOT
N/A

GOE
N/A

NOC
5243

O*NET-SOC
N/A

OVERVIEW

Photo styling is actually an all-encompassing term for the many and varied contributions that a *photo stylist* brings to the job. Primarily, the photo stylist works with a photographer to create a particular image, using props, backgrounds, accessories, clothing, costumes, food, linens, and other set elements. Much of the work exists within the print advertising industry, although stylists are also called to do film and commercial shoots. The photo stylist's resume can contain many specialties, from fashion to food, bridal to bathrooms, hair and makeup styling, to prop shopping and location searches. Some stylists may focus on one specialty; others may seek to maintain a wide repertoire of skills. While photo styling may seem like a vague and nebulous profession, it is an increasingly vital part of the photography and advertising industries.

HISTORY

Photo styling has existed since the first photographs were taken. Someone, whether a photographer, an assistant, a studio worker, a designer, or an editor, has to make sure all the elements within the frame are arranged in a certain way. Hair and makeup stylists in the film and publishing industries were probably the first to gain recognition (and credit). In fact, most people still associate "styling" exclusively with hair and makeup work, without fully appreciating the contribution of other stylists to the finished photo or film. To this day, photo styling credits are only occasionally listed in fashion and advertising spreads, but that trend is changing. Society is becoming more visually oriented, and the contributions made by stylists are becoming more important. Stylists are gaining the respect of people within the film, television, and print industries. Some photographer/stylist teams are as well known for their collaborative work as are actors and directors. After toiling in relative obscurity for many years, photo stylists are emerging as powerful voices in industry and in society.

THE JOB

The photo stylist is a creative collaborator, working with photographers, art directors, models, design houses, and clients to produce a visual image, usually for commercial purposes. It is both a technical and artistic occupation. The kind of work a photo stylist performs depends on, among other things, the nature of the photography; the needs of the photographer, studio, and art director; and the requests of the client. Because these factors vary from one situation to another, it is impossible to list all the aspects of a photo stylist's job. In simple terms, what a stylist does is help to create a "look." The specifics of how it is done are far more complicated. Moreover, "photo styling" itself is a very general term—there are many kinds of styling, almost as many as there are reasons for taking a photograph.

Prop gathering and set decoration are the most common assignments in photo styling, but many subspecialties exist within the field, each requiring different skills and experience. For example, fashion, wardrobe, and portrait shoots often require a number of professional stylists on hand to scout locations, prepare the set, acquire clothes and accessories, dress the models, and style hair and makeup.

Food stylists employ a variety of techniques, such as painting and glazing, to make everything from a bowl of cereal to a crawfish étouffée appear especially appetizing.

Home furnishings and domestic items specialists often introduce various props to give a natural look to the photographic set.

On-figure stylists fit clothes to a model, and *off-figure stylists* arrange clothes in attractive stacks or against an interesting background.

Soft-goods stylists introduce appropriate fabric, linens, and clothing into a shoot. The *tabletop stylist* may use anything from glue to Vaseline to give an added allure to a set of socket wrenches. *Hair and makeup stylists* are almost invariably cosmetic specialists, and are usually present on any set that employs live models.

Casting stylists locate modeling talent. Other stylists specialize in set design, child photography, bedding, bridal, and catalogs.

Many stylists are adept in more than one area, making them difficult to categorize.

Stylists may also bring special talents to the set, like floral design, gift wrapping, model building, or antiquing. They usually have a "bag of tricks" that will solve problems or create certain effects; a stylist's work kit might include everything from duct tape and cotton wadding to C-clamps and salt shakers. Sometimes a photo stylist is called on to design and build props, perform on-set, last-minute tailoring, even coordinate the entire production from the location search to crew accommodations. The most successful stylists will adapt to the needs of the job, and if they can't produce something themselves, they will know in an instant how and where to find someone who can. Versatility and flexibility are key attributes no matter what the stylist's specialty.

Being prepared for every possible situation is a large part of the photo stylist's job. Knowledge of photographic techniques, especially lighting, lenses, and filters, can help a stylist communicate better with the photographer. An understanding of the advertising industry and familiarity with specific product lines and designers, are also good tools for working with clients.

Organization is another vital aspect of the photo stylist's job. Before the shoot, the stylist must be sure that everything needed has been found and will arrive on time at the studio or location. During the shoot, even while working on a model or set, the stylist must be sure that all borrowed materials are being treated with care and that preparations for the next shot are underway. Afterwards, he or she must return items and maintain receipts and records, so as to keep the project within budget. The freelance stylist does all this while also rounding up new assignments and maintaining a current portfolio.

Only part of the stylist's time is spent in photo studios or on location. Much of the work is done on the phone and on the street, preparing for the job by gathering props and materials, procuring clothes, contacting models, or renting furniture. For the freelancer, lining up future employment can be a job in itself. A senior stylist working in-house at a magazine may have additional editorial duties, including working with art directors to introduce concepts and compose advertising narratives.

Even during downtime, the stylist must keep an eye out for ways to enhance his or her marketability. The chance discovery of a new boutique or specialty shop on the way to the grocery store can provide the stylist with a valuable new resource for later assignments. Maintaining a personal directory of resources is as essential as keeping a portfolio. Staying abreast of current trends and tastes through the media is also important, especially in the areas of fashion and lifestyle.

What a stylist does on the job largely depends on his or her unique talents and abilities. Photo stylists with the most experience and creative resources will make the greatest contribution to a project. As a premier stylist, that contribution extends beyond the set to society as a whole: shaping its tastes, making its images, and creating art that defines the era.

A clothing photo stylist preps shorts for photography. *(Terry Wild Stock)*

REQUIREMENTS

High School

You can take a number of classes to help prepare for this career while you are still in high school. Enroll in visual arts classes to learn about design and composition. Develop your hand-eye coordination in sculpture or pottery classes where you will be producing three-dimensional objects. Painting classes will teach you about colors, and photography classes will give you a familiarity using this medium. Skill with fabric is a must, so take family and consumer science classes that concentrate on fabric work. You will be able to cultivate your skills pressing and steaming clothes, doing minor alterations, and completing needlework. Because your work as a photo stylist may require you to work as a freelancer (running your own business), take mathematics classes or business and accounting classes that will prepare you to keep your own financial records. Of course, English classes are important to give you the communication skills that you will need to work well with a variety of people, to promote your own work, and to drum up new business.

Postsecondary Training

There is no specific postsecondary educational or training route you must take to enter this field. Some photo stylists have attended art schools, receiving degrees in photography. Others have entered the field by going into retail, working for large department stores, for example, to gain experience with advertising, marketing, and even product display. The Association of Stylists and Coordinators (ASC) recommends entering the field by working as an assistant for an established stylist. According to the ASC, such an informal apprenticeship usually lasts about two years. By then, the assistant typically has enough skills and connections to begin working on his or her own.

   If you are interested in a specialized type of styling, you may want to consider gaining experience in that area. For example, if hair and makeup styling interests you, take classes at a local cosmetology school to learn how to work with different kinds of hair. If food styling interests you, attend cooking or baking classes at a culinary school. Again, this will give you experience working with the materials to be photographed. It is essential to have a knowledge of photography for this work, so continue to take photography classes to build your skills. Advertising courses may also be useful.

Other Requirements

The personal qualities most sought in a photo stylist are creativity, taste, resourcefulness, and good instincts. Stylists work with a variety of people, such as clients, models, and prop suppliers, and therefore they need to have a calm and supportive personality. Schedules can be hectic and work is not always done during normal business hours, so stylists need flexibility, the ability to work under pressure, and patience. Stylists who are easy to work with often find that they have a large number of clients. An eye for detail is a must. Stylists are responsible for making sure that everything appearing in a photo—from a model's hairstyle to the size and color of a lamp—is exactly right.

The specialties employed for certain shoots require a familiarity with, for instance, food preparation, home decorating, children, formal attire, bedding, and any number of other potential subjects. A photo stylist, like any artist, draws from his or her own experience for inspiration, so exposure to a wide variety of experiences will benefit anyone entering the field.

EXPLORING

There are a number of fun ways to explore your interest in this career. Try teaming up with a friend to conduct your own photo shoot. Arm yourself with a camera, decide on a location (inside or outside), gather some props or costumes, and take a series of photographs. At a professional level, these are known as test shots and are used to build up the portfolios of photographers, models, and stylists. But a backyard photo shoot can be a good way to appreciate the elements involved with this career. Obviously, any opportunity to visit a real photographer's set can be an invaluable learning experience; ask a guidance counselor to help you arrange such a field trip. You should also consider joining a photography or art club. Besides giving you the opportunity to work with the medium, such clubs may also sponsor talks or meetings with professionals in the field.

Look for part-time or summer work in the retail field where you may have the opportunity to set up displays and learn about advertising. Even if you can't find such work, watch someone prepare a display in a department store window. Many stylists start out as window dressers or doing in-store display work.

EMPLOYERS

Relatively few positions are available for full-time, salaried photo stylists. Some ad agencies, magazines, and companies that sell their merchandise through catalogs have stylists on staff. Most photo stylists, however, work as freelancers. They are hired for individual assignments by photographers, ad agencies, design firms, catalog houses, and any other enterprise that uses photographic services.

STARTING OUT

A person can enter the field of photo styling at any point in life, but there is no clear-cut way to go about it. Some people, if they have the resources, hire photographers to shoot a portfolio with them, then shop it around to production houses and other photographers. However, most prospective employers prefer that a stylist has previous on-set experience.

As the ASC recommends, one of the best ways to break into this field is to find work as a stylist's assistant. Production houses and photo studios that employ full-time stylists usually keep a directory of assistants. Most cities have a creative directory of established stylists who may need assistants. It is important to always leave a name and number; they may have no work available immediately, but might be desperate for help next month. Working as an assistant will provide you with important on-set experience as well as show you the nuts and bolts of the job—including the drudgery along with the rewards. Building a reputation is most important at any stage of this career, since most photographers find stylists by word of mouth and recommendations, in addition to reviewing portfolios. Assistants will also be introduced to the people who may hire them down the road as full-fledged stylists, giving them an opportunity to make a good impression. Eventually, you can seek out a photographer who needs a stylist and work together on test shots. Once you have enough examples of your work for a portfolio, you can show it to agents, editors, and photographers.

Agency representation can be of enormous help to the freelancer. An agent finds work for the stylist and pays him or her on a regular basis (after extracting an average commission of 20 percent). The benefits of representation is that while a stylist is working one job, the agent is lining up the next. Some agencies represent stylists exclusively; others also handle models, photographers, and actors.

ADVANCEMENT

Advancement in this field can be measured by the amount of bookings a stylist obtains, the steadiness of work, and a regularly increasing pay rate. It can also be determined by the quality of a stylist's clients, the reputation of the photographer, and the nature of the assignments. Some stylists start out with lower-end catalogs and work their way up. If the goal is to do high fashion, then the steps along the way will be readily apparent in the quality of the merchandise and the size of the client.

The opportunity to work with highly regarded photographers is also a step up, even if the stylist's pay rate remains the same. In a career built on reputation, experience with the industry's major players is priceless. Senior stylists at magazines often help in ad design and planning. Some stylists advance to become art directors and fashion editors. Ultimately, each stylist has his or her own goals in sight. The "rare-air" of high fashion and celebrity photography may not be the end-all for all stylists; a good steady income and the chance to work regularly with friendly, creative people may, in fact, be of more importance.

EARNINGS

Like almost everything else in this field, earning potential varies from one stylist to the next. Salaries at production houses can start as low as $8 an hour, but usually include fringe benefits like health insurance, not to mention a regular paycheck. The freelancer, on the other hand, has enormous earning potential. An experienced fashion or food stylist can demand as much as $800 or more a day, depending on his or her reputation and the budget of the production. Regular bookings at this level, along with travel and accommodation costs (almost always paid for), translate into a substantial income.

Most photo stylists, however, earn less and average approximately $350 to $500 per day. According to the ASC, assistant stylists, who are hired by the day, can expect to make approximately $150 to $200 per day. Neither assistants nor stylists who are freelancers receive any benefits. They must provide for their own health insurance and retirement, and they receive no pay for sick days or vacation time. In addition, while a stylist may have a job that pays $500 a day for several days, the stylist may also have unpaid periods when he or she is looking for the next assignment.

WORK ENVIRONMENT

Work conditions for a photo stylist are as varied as the job itself. Preparation for a shoot may involve hours on the telephone, calling from the home or office, and more hours shopping for props and materials to use on the set. Much of the work is done inside comfortable photo studios or at other indoor locations, but sometimes, especially in fashion and catalog photography, outdoor locations are also used. If the merchandise is of a seasonal nature, this could mean long days working in a cold field photographing winter parkas against a snowy background, or it could mean flying down to Key

West in January for a week shooting next summer's line of swimwear. Travel, both local and long distance, is part of the job. Days can be long, from dawn to dusk, or they may require the stylist's presence for only a few hours on the set. Hours vary, but a stylist must always be flexible, especially the freelancer who may be called in on a day's notice.

Regardless of whether stylists own or rent photo and prop equipment, they must be prepared to put out a lot of their own money. Most clients and studios budget for these expenses and reimburse the stylist, but the initial funds must sometimes come from the stylist's own pocket. Maintaining a portfolio, purchasing equipment, and paying agents' fees may also add to the cost of doing business.

Photo styling can be an extremely lucrative career, but there is no assurance that a stylist will find steady employment. It is wise to establish an emergency fund in the event that work disappears for a time. Busy periods often correspond to seasonal advertising campaigns and film work. A stylist might have a great year followed by a disappointing one.

Stress levels vary from one assignment to the next. Some shoots may go smoothly, others may have a crisis occur every minute. Stylists must be able to remain calm and resilient in the face of enormous pressure. Personality clashes may also occur despite every effort to avoid them, adding to the stress of the job. For the freelancer, the pressure to find new work and maintain proper business records are still further sources of stress. Photo stylists will also spend considerable time on their feet, stooping and kneeling in uncomfortable positions or trying to get something aligned just right. They also may need to transport heavy material and merchandise to and from the studio or location or move these elements around the set during the shoot. Reliable transportation is essential.

The irregular hours of a photo stylist can be an attraction for people who enjoy variety in their lives. Work conditions are not always that strenuous. The work can also be pleasant and fun, as the crew trades jokes and experiences, solves problems together, and shares the excitement of a sudden inspiration. The rewards of working with a team of professionals on an interesting, creative project is a condition of the job that most stylists treasure.

OUTLOOK

The value of a good photo stylist is becoming more and more apparent to photographers and advertising clients. However, the outlook for employment for stylists depends a great deal on their perseverance and reputation. Although photo studios can be found in nearly every community, larger cities are the most fertile places to find work. The fortunes of the stylist are intrinsically related to the health of the advertising, film, video, and commercial photography industries—all of which are in good shape. Stylists should try, however, to maintain a wide client base so they can be assured of regular work in case one source dries up.

Technological advances, especially in the areas of digital photography and photo enhancement, may transform, but not eliminate, the role of the photo stylist in the future. Someday there may be educational avenues for the stylist to enter into the field, and this may increase the amount of competition for styling assignments. Ultimately, though, maintaining quality work is the best insurance for continued employment.

FOR MORE INFORMATION

For information on the career of photo stylist, contact
Association of Stylists and Coordinators
18 East 18th Street, #5E
New York, NY 10003-1933
Email: info@stylistsasc.com
http://www.stylistsasc.com

To see examples of professional photography and read about news in the field, check out the following publication and Web site:
Photo District News
770 Broadway, 7th Floor
New York, NY 10003-9522
Tel: 646-654-5780
http://www.pdn-pix.com

INTERVIEW

Carey Cornelius, a California-based photo stylist, has worked for such well-known companies as Old Navy/Gap, Land's End, Macy's, Dockers/Levis, and Disney. (Visit http://www.thephotostylist.com to see samples of her work.) Carey discussed her career with the editors of *Careers in Focus: Advertising and Marketing.*

Q. Please tell us about your business.

A. I am a photo stylist who is part of a creative team that puts together the photographic images used to sell products. These can be anything from clothing, accessories, bedding, furniture, etc. My job is to execute the creative vision of the art director and/or creative director and ultimately enable the client to successfully sell and make their product attractive to the consumer. Many people are not aware of this little niche in advertising. I am the liaison between the photographer and the art director. I gather, which means shop or "hunt" for, the various elements that will be used in the photo shoots and then arrange them to be photographed. I especially like working on clothing and bedding shoots.

Q. Why did you decide to become a photo stylist?

A. I don't think early on I "decided" to become a stylist. I had worked in entertainment for Disneyland for 16 years and obtained my degree in illustration art and advertising design (now called graphic design). So somewhere between putting on or coordinating shows at Disney and then having an art background, I met a stylist who needed an assistant. The job was not glamorous and it was a lot of ironing and steaming clothes ("prepping"), and did I mention the jobs were in central Mexico and there were at least 22 large bags that I had to get through customs with official forms and a lot of luck. At 23 years old I had no idea that 18 years later this would become my career. The more jobs I did, the more confident and knowledgeable I became about this industry. It truly was on-the-job training. In about two years, I was able to transition from assisting to being a photo stylist. I worked on all sorts of photo styling jobs.

   The reason why I chose to be a photo stylist is because I love the art of presentation. I enjoy taking an ordinary product that maybe most people would pass over and coming up with a creative solution or way of displaying it so that it is desirable. I love that I am freelance and each job is a new project, a new direction and inspiration. I love working with creative and energetic people and also, on occasion, the opportunities to travel to the world's most beautiful locations.

Q. Take us through a day in your life as a photo stylist. What are your typical tasks/responsibilities?

A. There is really not a typical day as a photo stylist since no two jobs or clients are alike. But, I will describe a common scenario. Let's say I was going to shoot bedding. I would usually have a meeting and brainstorm with the client and art director to discuss what would be the best way to photograph and sell the bedding. Usually, the concept for the photo shoot is an "overall" feeling or "vision." I then go away with this idea and write down everything I can think of that we will need for the day of the shoot. I start breaking it down. Sometimes when I am out shopping (hunting), I find things or am inspired, and this is how I begin pulling together a more detailed tangible direction.

Days on location and studio days can be very different. My day of "prepping" can mean simple props and flowers or renting furniture and walls. On the day of the shoot, we meet in the morning to discuss our game plan. There are usually anywhere between six and 20 shots to be accomplished. I then arrange the product or bedding in this case to best display all the special features and, of course, how it looks best. I usually have a shape (vertical, horizontal, or square) that the photographic image needs to be. (Let's say the image was going to be used for the front cover of a catalog, it would need to be somewhat vertical.) The photographer does his part, and then the art director signs off on it. (They usually have input on both how it is styled and the way it is photographed.) Then when everyone agrees that it looks fabulous, we move on to the next shot.

Q. What do you like most and least about your job?
A. The things that I like least about my job are that on some days it is a lot of work and can be stressful when I can't find what I am looking for. In my head, I know what it needs to be but I can't locate it anywhere! Pumpkins in the off-season or beach balls in the winter are a common request. (I have learned to stock these items in my garage!) This job can consist of very early mornings and long days. It is also a job in a very subjective industry. I may think something is great and someone else may strongly object. (That does not happen very often though.) Overall, I love 90 percent of everything else. I enjoy the process of concepting and the "hands-on" aspect of moving things around the set to find just the right solution. And finally, at the end of the day it is such a good feeling to feel proud of my work and I can say, wow, that really looks good.

Q. What advice would you give to high school students who are interested in this career?
A. I would say if anyone wanted to become a photo stylist that they should have several strengths. First, they should have an art/design background of color, composition, and style. Secondly, to have a "MacGyver" personality (resourceful)—where if you can't find it, you can make it (really)! Finally, it is networking and whom you know in the industry.

You really need to try to assist a stylist and get on-the-job training. There are no classes available that I'm aware of for this small niche in advertising. If you have some art classes under your belt, you have a problem-solving personality, and hook up with a strong working photo stylist, you will be on your way! I would start by volunteering to help set up shots and/or prop shopping for photographers. I've received many jobs from loyal photographers who remember I was hard working and did a good job.

I feel very fortunate to have found such a fulfilling, creative, and flexible career.

Photographers

OVERVIEW

Photographers take and sometimes develop and print pictures of people, places, objects, and events, using a variety of cameras and photographic equipment. They work in the advertising, marketing, publishing, public relations, science, and business industries, as well as provide personal photographic services. They may also work as fine artists. There are approximately 122,000 photographers employed in the United States.

HISTORY

The word photograph means "to write with light." Although the art of photography dates back only about 150 years, the two Greek words that were chosen and combined to refer to this skill quite accurately describe it.

The discoveries that led eventually to photography began early in the 18th century when German scientist Dr. Johann H. Schultze, experimented with the action of light on certain chemicals. He found that when these chemicals were covered by dark paper, they did not change color, but when they were exposed to sunlight, they darkened. The French painter Louis Daguerre became the first photographer in 1839, using silver-iodide-coated plates and a small box. To develop images on the plates, Daguerre exposed them to mercury vapor. The daguerreotype, as these early photographs came to be known, took minutes to expose and the developing process was directly to the plate. There were no prints made.

Although the daguerreotype was the sensation of its day, it was not until George Eastman invented a simple camera and flexible roll film that photography began to come into widespread use in the late 1800s. After exposing this film to light and developing it with chemicals, the film revealed a color-reversed image, called a negative. To make the negative positive (that is, print a picture), light must be shone through the negative on to light-sensitive paper. This process can be repeated to make multiple copies of an image from one negative.

One of the most important developments in recent years is digital photography. In digital photography, instead of using film, pictures are recorded on microchips, which can then be downloaded onto a computer's hard drive. The images can be manipulated in size, color, and shape, virtually eliminating the need for a darkroom.

New methods (such as digital photography) and new creative mediums (such as the Internet) have created many new opportunities for photographers, including those employed by advertising and marketing firms, public relations firms, corporations, nonprofit organizations, and government agencies.

THE JOB

Commercial and advertising photographers shoot photographs that will be seen in magazines, on billboards, in promotional materials of various kinds, and in catalogs, among many other places. This branch of photography requires a very high level of technical skill since quality is of paramount importance. A photographer who photographs a product for an advertising campaign, for example, must be able to make that product look irresistibly attractive and perfect in every way. Any flaw in the photo would defeat the purpose of the advertising. The commercial field includes specializations such as food, fashion, product, and industrial photography. Commercial photographers often employ *photo stylists*, who collect props, prepare sets, and arrange products to be shot. (See the Photo Stylists article for more information.)

Photography is both an artistic and technical occupation. There are many variables in the process that a knowledgeable photographer can manipulate to produce a clear image or a more abstract work of fine art. First, photographers know how to use cameras and can adjust focus, shutter speeds, aperture, lenses, and filters. They know about the types and speeds of films. Photographers also know about light and shadow, deciding when to use available natural light and when to set up artificial lighting to achieve desired effects.

Some photographers who work with still photography send their film to laboratories, while others develop their own negatives and make their own prints. These processes require knowledge of chemicals such as developers and fixers and how to use enlarging equipment. Photographers must also be familiar with the large variety of papers available for printing photographs, all of which deliver a different effect. Most photographers continually experiment with photographic processes to improve their technical proficiency or to create special effects.

With the new technology of digital photography, film is replaced by microchips that record pictures in digital format, which can then be downloaded onto a computer's hard drive. Using special software, photographers can manipulate the images on the screen and place them directly onto the layout of a Web site or brochure.

Some photographers write for trade and technical journals, teach photography in schools and colleges, act as representatives of photographic equipment manufacturers, sell photographic equipment and supplies, produce documentary films, or do freelance work.

REQUIREMENTS

High School

While in high school, take as many art and photography classes that are available. Chemistry is useful for understanding developing and printing processes. You can learn about photo manipulation software and digital photography in computer classes; business classes will help if you are considering a freelance career.

Postsecondary Training

A college education is not required to become a photographer, although college training probably offers the most promising assurance of success in fields such as advertising, industrial, news, or scientific photography. There are degree programs at the associate's, bachelor's, and master's levels. Many men and women, however, become photographers with no formal education beyond high school.

To become a photographer, you should have a broad technical understanding of photography plus as much practical experience with cameras as possible. Take many different kinds of photographs with a variety of cameras and subjects. Learn how to develop photographs and, if possible, build your own darkroom or rent one.

A photographer takes photos of professional tennis player Maria Sharapova during a photo shoot for a watch company advertising campaign. *(Stefano Paltera, AP Images)*

Experience in picture composition, cropping prints (cutting images to a desired size), enlarging, and retouching are all valuable. Learn how to use digital cameras and photo editing software.

Certification or Licensing

The Professional Photographic Certification Commission, which is affiliated with Professional Photographers of America, offers certification to photographers who have had their creative work reviewed by a panel of judges and passed a written exam that tests their technical expertise. Visit http://certifiedphotographer.com for more information.

Other Requirements

You should possess manual dexterity, good eyesight and color vision, and artistic ability to succeed in this line of work. You need an eye for form and line, an appreciation of light and shadow, and the ability to use imaginative and creative approaches to photographs or film, especially in commercial work. In addition, you should be patient and accurate and enjoy working with detail.

Self-employed (or freelance) photographers need good business skills. They must be able to manage their own studios, including hiring and managing assistants and other employees, keeping records, and maintaining photographic and business files. Marketing and sales skills are also important to a successful freelance photography business.

EXPLORING

Photography is a field that anyone with a camera can explore. To learn more about this career, enter photography contests or join the high school camera club, yearbook or newspaper staffs, and community hobby groups. You can also seek a part-time or summer job in a camera shop or work as a developer in a laboratory or processing center.

EMPLOYERS

About 122,000 photographers work in the United States, more than half of whom are self-employed. Most jobs for photographers are provided by photographic or commercial art studios; other employers include newspapers and magazines, radio and TV stations, government agencies, advertising and marketing firms, and manufacturing companies. Colleges, universities, and other educational institutions employ photographers to prepare promotional and educational materials.

STARTING OUT

Some photographers enter the field as apprentices, trainees, or assistants. Trainees may work in a darkroom, camera shop, or developing laboratory. They may move lights and arrange backgrounds for a commercial or portrait photographer or motion picture photographer. Assistants spend many months learning this kind of work before they move into a job behind a camera.

Many large cities have schools of photography, which may be a good way to start in the field. Other photographers choose to go into business for themselves as soon as they have finished their formal education. Setting up a studio may not require a large capital outlay, but beginners may find that success does not come easily.

ADVANCEMENT

Because photography is such a diversified field, there is no usual way in which to get ahead. Those who begin by working for someone may advance to owning their own businesses. Commercial photographers may gain prestige as more of their pictures are placed in well-known trade journals or popular magazines. A few photographers may become celebrities in their own right by making contributions to the art world or the sciences.

EARNINGS

The U.S. Department of Labor reports that salaried photographers earned median annual salaries of $26,170 in 2006. Salaries ranged from less than $15,540 to more than $56,640. Photographers who were employed by newspaper, book, and directory publishers earned mean annual salaries of $37,800 in 2006, while those employed by colleges and universities earned $40,990.

Photographers in salaried jobs usually receive benefits such as paid holidays, vacations, and sick leave and medical insurance.

Self-employed photographers often earn more than salaried photographers, but their earnings depend on general business conditions. In addition, self-employed photographers do not receive the benefits that a company provides its employees.

WORK ENVIRONMENT

Work conditions vary based on the job and employer. Many photographers work a 35- to 40-hour workweek, but freelancers and news photographers often put in long, irregular hours. Commercial and portrait photographers work in comfortable surroundings. Photojournalists seldom are assured physical comfort in their work and may in fact face danger when covering stories on natural disasters or military conflicts. Some photographers work in research laboratory settings; others work on aircraft; and still others work underwater. For some photographers, conditions change from day to day. They may be photographing a hot and dusty rodeo one day, and taking pictures of a dog sled race in Alaska the next.

In general, photographers work under pressure to meet deadlines and satisfy customers. Freelance photographers have the added pressure of uncertain incomes and have to continually seek out new clients.

For specialists in fields such as fashion photography, breaking into the field may take years. Working as another photographer's assistant is physically demanding when carrying equipment is required.

For freelance photographers, the cost of equipment can be quite expensive, with no assurance that the money spent will be repaid through income from future assignments. Freelancers in travel-related photography, such as travel and tourism photographers and photojournalists, have the added cost of transportation and accommodations. For all photographers, flexibility is a major asset.

OUTLOOK

Employment of photographers will increase about as fast as the average for all occupations through 2016, according to the *Occupational Outlook Handbook*. The demand for new images should remain strong in education, communication, entertainment, marketing, and research. As the Internet grows and more newspapers and magazines turn to electronic publishing, demand will increase for photographers to produce digital images.

Photography is a highly competitive field. There are far more photographers than positions available. Only those who are extremely talented and highly skilled can support themselves as self-employed photographers. Many photographers take pictures as a sideline while working another job.

FOR MORE INFORMATION

For information on careers in advertising photography, contact
Advertising Photographers of America
PO Box 250
White Plains, NY 10605-0250
Tel: 800-272-6264
http://www.apanational.com

This organization provides training, offers certification, publishes its own magazine, and sponsors various services for its members.
Professional Photographers of America
229 Peachtree Street, NE, Suite 2200
Atlanta, GA 30303-1608
Tel: 800-786-6277
Email: csc@ppa.com
http://www.ppa.com

For information on opportunities in photography for women, contact
Professional Women Photographers
511 Avenue of the Americas, #138
New York, NY 10011-8436

Email: info@pwponline.org
http://www.pwponline.org

For information on student membership, contact
Student Photographic Society
229 Peachtree Street, NE, Suite 2200
Atlanta, GA 30303-1608
Tel: 866-886-5325
Email: info@studentphoto.com
http://www.studentphoto.com

Public Opinion Researchers

OVERVIEW

Public opinion researchers help measure public sentiment about various products, services, or social issues by gathering information from a sample of the population through questionnaires and interviews. They collect, analyze, and interpret data and opinions to explore issues and forecast trends. Their poll results help businesspeople, politicians, and other decision makers determine what's on the public's mind. It is estimated that there are fewer than 100,000 full-time workers currently in the field, primarily employed by the government or private industry in large cities.

HISTORY

Public opinion research began in a rudimentary way in the 1830s and 1840s when local newspapers asked readers to fill out unofficial ballots indicating for whom they had voted in a particular election. Since that time, research on political issues has been conducted with increasing frequency—especially during presidential election years. However, public opinion research is most widely used by businesses to determine what products or services consumers like or dislike.

As questionnaires and interviewing techniques have become more refined, the field of public opinion research has become more accurate at reflecting individual attitudes and opinions of the sample groups. Companies like The Gallup Organization and Harris Interactive conduct surveys for a wide range of political and economic purposes. Although some people

QUICK FACTS

School Subjects
Business
Mathematics
Psychology

Personal Skills
Communication/ideas
Technical/scientific

Work Environment
Indoors and outdoors
Primarily multiple locations

Minimum Education Level
Bachelor's degree

Salary Range
$16,720 to $58,820 to
$112,510+

Certification or Licensing
None available

Outlook
Much faster than the average

DOT
205

GOE
02.04.02

NOC
1454

O*NET-SOC
19-3021.00, 19-3022.00

continue to question the accuracy and importance of polls, they have become an integral part of our social fabric.

THE JOB

Public opinion researchers conduct interviews and gather data that accurately reflect public opinions. They do this so decision makers in the business and political worlds have a better idea of what people want on a wide range of issues. Public opinion is sometimes gauged by interviewing a small percentage of the population containing a variety of people who closely parallel the larger population in terms of age, race, income, and other factors. At other times, researchers interview people who represent a certain demographic group. Public opinion researchers may help a company implement a new marketing strategy or help a political candidate decide which campaign issues the public considers important.

Researchers use a variety of methods to collect and analyze public opinion. The particular method depends on the target audience and the type of information desired. For example, if the owner of a shopping mall is interested in gauging the opinions of shoppers, the research company will most likely station interviewers in selected areas around the mall so they can question the shoppers. On the other hand, a public relations firm may be interested in the opinions of a particular demographic group, such as working mothers or teenagers. In this case, the research firm would plan a procedure (such as a telephone survey) providing access to that group. Other field collection methods include interviews in the home and at work as well as questionnaires that are filled out by respondents and then returned through the mail.

Planning is an important ingredient in developing an effective survey method. After they receive an assignment, researchers decide what portion of the population they will survey and develop questions that will result in an accurate gauging of opinion. Researchers investigate whether previous surveys have been done on a particular topic, and if so, what the results were.

It is important that exactly the same procedures be used throughout the entire data collection process so that the survey is not influenced by the individual styles of the interviewers. For this reason, the process is closely monitored by supervisory personnel. *Research assistants* help train survey interviewers, prepare survey questionnaires and related materials, and tabulate and code survey results.

Other specialists within the field include *marketing research analysts,* who collect, analyze, and interpret survey results to determine what they mean. They prepare reports and make recommendations on

A public opinion researcher (left) conducts a residential survey. *(Joseph Kaczmarek, AP Images)*

subjects ranging from preferences of prospective customers to future sales trends. They use mathematical and statistical models to analyze research. Research analysts are careful to screen out unimportant or invalid information that could skew their survey results. (For more information on this career, see the article Marketing Research Analysts.) Some research analysts specialize in one industry or area. For example, *agricultural marketing research analysts* prepare sales forecasts for food businesses, which use the information in their advertising and sales programs. *Survey workers* conduct public opinion interviews to determine people's buying habits or opinions on public issues. Survey workers contact people in their homes, at work, at random in public places, or via the telephone, questioning the person in a specified manner, usually following a questionnaire format.

At times public opinion researchers are mistaken for telemarketers. According to the Council for Marketing and Opinion Research, public opinion researchers are conducting serious research, collecting opinions whereas telemarketers ultimately are in the business of sales.

REQUIREMENTS

High School

Because the ability to communicate in both spoken and written form is crucial for this job, you should take courses in English, social studies, and speech arts while in high school. In addition, take mathematics (especially statistics) and any courses in journalism or psychology that are available. Knowledge of a foreign language is also helpful.

Postsecondary Training

A college degree in business administration or economics provides good background for public opinion researchers. A degree in sociology or psychology will be helpful for those interested in studying consumer demand or opinion research, while work in engineering or statistics might be more useful for those interested in certain types of industrial or analytical research.

Because of the increasingly sophisticated techniques used in public opinion research, most employers expect researchers to be familiar with computer applications, and many require a master's degree in business administration, educational psychology, political science, or sociology. While a doctorate is not necessary for most researchers, it is highly desirable for those who plan to become involved with complex research studies or work in an academic environment.

Other Requirements

Public opinion researchers who conduct interviews must be outgoing and enjoy interacting with a wide variety of people. Because much of the work involves getting people to reveal their personal opinions and beliefs, you must be a good listener and as nonjudgmental as possible. You must be patient and be able to handle rejection because some people may be uncooperative during the interviewing process.

If you choose to work in data analysis, you should be able to pay close attention to detail and spend long hours analyzing complex data. You may experience some pressure when forced to collect data or solve a problem within a specified period of time. If you intend to plan questionnaires, you will need good analytical skills and a strong command of the English language.

EXPLORING

High school students can often work as survey workers for a telemarketing firm or other consumer research company. Work opportunities may also be available to learn about the coding and tabulation of survey data. Actual participation in a consumer survey may also offer insight into the type of work involved in the field. You should also try to talk with professionals already working in the field to learn more about the profession.

EMPLOYERS

Fewer than 100,000 full-time public opinion researchers are employed in the field. Public opinion workers are primarily employed by private companies, such as public and private research firms and advertising agencies. They also work for the government and for colleges and universities, often in research and teaching capacities. As is usually the case, those with the most experience and education should find the greatest number of job opportunities. Gaining experience in a specific area (such as food products) can give prospective researchers an edge.

STARTING OUT

Many people enter the field in a support position such as a survey worker, and with experience become interviewers or work as data analysts. Those with applicable education, training, and experience may begin as interviewers or data analysts. College career services counselors can often help qualified students find an appropriate position in public opinion research. Contacts can also be made through summer employment or by locating public and private research companies in the phone book and on the Web.

ADVANCEMENT

Advancement opportunities are numerous in the public opinion research field. Often a research assistant will be promoted to a position as an interviewer or data analyst and, after sufficient experience in these or other aspects of research project development, become involved in a supervisory or planning capacity.

With a master's degree or doctorate, a person can become a manager of a large private research organization or marketing research director for an industrial or business firm. Those with extended work experience in public opinion research and with sufficient credentials may choose to start their own companies. Opportunities also exist in university teaching or research and development.

EARNINGS

Starting salaries vary according to the skill and experience of the applicant, the nature of the position, and the size of the company. While the U.S. Department of Labor (USDL) does not offer salary information for public opinion researchers, it does report that market research analysts (a type of public opinion researcher) earned a median salary of $58,820 in 2006. Earnings ranged from less than $32,250 to $112,510 or more. The USDL also reports that survey workers earned salaries that ranged from less than $16,720 to more than $73,630 in 2006. The median annual salary for survey workers was $33,360 in 2006. Those in academic positions may earn somewhat less than their counterparts in the business community, but federal government salaries are competitive with those in the private sector.

Most full-time public opinion researchers receive the usual medical, pension, vacation, and other benefits enjoyed by other professional workers. Managers may also receive bonuses based on their company's performance.

WORK ENVIRONMENT

Public opinion researchers usually work a standard 40-hour week, although they may have to work overtime occasionally if a project has a tight deadline. Those in supervisory positions may work especially long hours overseeing the collection and interpretation of information.

When conducting telephone interviews or organizing or analyzing data, researchers work in comfortable offices, with calculators, computers, and data processing equipment close at hand. When collecting information via personal interviews or questionnaires, it is not unusual to spend time outside in shopping malls, on the street, or in private homes. Some evening and weekend work may be involved because people are most readily available to be interviewed at those times. Some research positions may include assignments that involve travel, but these are generally short assignments.

OUTLOOK

According to the U.S. Department of Labor, employment of market and survey research workers is expected to grow faster than the average for all occupations through 2016. Opportunities for market research specialists who work in advertising and related industries will be even better, with employment predicted to grow by more than 24 percent (or much faster than the average) through 2016. Job opportunities should be ample for those trained in public opinion research, particularly if they have graduate degrees. Those who specialize in marketing, mathematics, and statistics will have the best opportunities. Marketing research firms, financial services organizations, health care institutions, advertising firms, public relations firms, and insurance firms are potential employers.

FOR MORE INFORMATION

For more information on market research, contact
Advertising Research Foundation
432 Park Avenue South
New York, NY 10016-8013
Tel: 212-751-5656
Email: info@thearf.org
http://www.arfsite.org

For information on graduate programs, contact
American Association for Public Opinion Research
PO Box 14263
Lenexa, KS 66285-4263
Tel: 913-895-4601
Email: info@aapor.org
http://www.aapor.org

For career development information, contact
American Marketing Association
311 South Wacker Drive, Suite 5800
Chicago, IL 60606-6629
Tel: 800-262-1150
http://www.marketingpower.com

For comprehensive information on market and opinion research, contact
Council for Marketing and Opinion Research
110 National Drive, 2nd Floor
Glastonbury, CT 06033-1212
Tel: 860-657-1881
Email: information@cmor.org
http://www.cmor.org

For information on survey research and graduate programs, contact
Council of American Survey Research Organizations
170 North Country Road, Suite 4
Port Jefferson, NY 11777-2606

Tel: 631-928-6954
Email: casro@casro.org
http://www.casro.org

For career information, contact
Marketing Research Association
110 National Drive, 2nd Floor
Glastonbury, CT 06033-1212
Tel: 860-682-1000
Email: email@mra-net.org
http://www.mra-net.org

The following companies are leaders in survey and marketing research:
The Gallup Organization
http://www.gallup.com

Harris Interactive
http://www.harrisinteractive.com

Public Relations Specialists

OVERVIEW

Public relations (PR) specialists develop and maintain programs that present a favorable public image for an individual or organization. They provide information to the target audience (generally, the public at large) about the client, its goals and accomplishments, and any further plans or projects that may be of public interest.

PR specialists may be employed by corporations, government agencies, nonprofit organizations—almost any type of organization. Many PR specialists hold positions in public relations consulting firms or work for advertising agencies. There are approximately 29,000 public relations specialists employed in advertising and related industries in the United States.

HISTORY

The first public relations counsel was a reporter Ivy Ledbetter Lee, who in 1906 was named press representative for coal mine operators. Labor disputes were becoming a large concern of the operators, and they had run into problems because of their continual refusal to talk to the press and the hired miners. Lee convinced the mine operators to start responding to press questions and supply the press with information on the mine activities.

During and after World War II, the rapid advancement of communications techniques prompted firms to realize they needed professional help to ensure their messages were given proper public attention.

Manufacturing firms that had turned their production facilities over to the war effort returned to the manufacture of peacetime products and enlisted the aid of public relations professionals to forcefully bring products and the company name before the buying public.

Large business firms, labor unions, and service organizations, such as the American Red Cross, Boy Scouts of America, and the YMCA, began to recognize the value of establishing positive, healthy relationships with the public that they served and depended on for support. The need for effective public relations was often emphasized when circumstances beyond a company's or institution's control created unfavorable reaction from the public.

Public relations specialists must be experts at representing their clients before the media. The rapid growth of the public relations field since 1945 is testimony to the increased awareness in all industries of the need for professional attention to the proper use of media and the public relations approach to the many publics of a firm or an organization—customers, employees, stockholders, contributors, and competitors.

THE JOB

Public relations specialists are employed to do a variety of tasks. They may be employed primarily as *writers,* creating reports, news releases, and booklet texts. Others write speeches or create copy for radio, TV, or film sequences. These workers often spend much of their time contacting the press, radio, and TV as well as magazines on behalf of the employer. Some PR specialists work more as *editors* than writers, fact-checking and rewriting employee publications, newsletters, shareholder reports, and other management communications.

Specialists may choose to concentrate in graphic design, using their background knowledge of art and layout to develop brochures, booklets, and photographic communications. Other PR workers handle special events, such as press parties, convention exhibits, open houses, or anniversary celebrations.

PR specialists must be alert to any and all company or institutional events that are newsworthy. They prepare news releases and direct them toward the proper media. Specialists working for manufacturers and retailers are concerned with efforts that will promote sales and create goodwill for the firm's products. They work closely with the marketing and sales departments in announcing new products, preparing displays, and attending occasional dealers' conventions.

Books to Read

Mogel, Leonard. *Making It in Public Relations: An Insider's Guide to Career Opportunities.* 2d ed. New York: Lawrence Erlbaum, 2002.

Seitel, Fraser P. *The Practice of Public Relations.* 10th ed. Upper Saddle River, N.J.: Prentice Hall, 2006.

Vault Editors. *Vault Guide to the Top Advertising & Public Relations Employers.* New York: Vault Inc., 2008.

Yaverbaum, Eric, Ilese Benun, and Bob Bly. *Public Relations for Dummies.* New York: For Dummies, 2006.

Zappala, Joseph M., and Ann R. Carden. *Public Relations Worktext: A Writing and Planning Resource.* 2d ed. New York: Lawrence Erlbaum, 2004.

A large firm may have a *director of public relations* who is a vice president of the company and in charge of a staff that includes writers, artists, researchers, and other specialists. Publicity for an individual or a small organization may involve many of the same areas of expertise but may be carried out by a few people or possibly even one person.

Many PR workers act as consultants (rather than staff) of a corporation, association, college, hospital, or other institution. These workers have the advantage of being able to operate independently, state opinions objectively, and work with more than one type of business or association.

PR specialists are called on to work with the public opinion aspects of almost every corporate or institutional problem—ranging from the opening of a new manufacturing plant to a college's dormitory dedication to a merger or sale of a company.

Public relations professionals may specialize. *Lobbyists* try to persuade legislators and other officeholders to pass laws favoring the interests of the firms or people they represent. *Fund-raising directors* develop and direct programs designed to raise funds for social welfare agencies and other nonprofit organizations.

Early in their careers, public relations specialists become accustomed to having others receive credit for their behind-the-scenes work. The speeches they draft will be delivered by company officers, the magazine articles they prepare may be attributed to the president of the company, and they may be consulted to prepare the message

A public relations specialist answers reporters' questions during a press conference. *(Tom & Dee McCarthy, Corbis)*

to stockholders from the chairman of the board that appears in the annual report.

REQUIREMENTS

High School

While in high school, take courses in English, humanities, journalism, languages, and public speaking because public relations is based on effective communication with others. Courses such as these will develop your skills in written and oral communication as well as provide a better understanding of different fields and industries to be publicized.

Postsecondary Training

Most people employed in public relations have a college degree. Major fields of study most beneficial to developing the proper skills are English, journalism, and public relations. Some employers feel that majoring in the area in which the public relations person will eventually work is the best training. A knowledge of business administration is most helpful as is a native talent for selling. A graduate degree may be required for managerial positions. People with a bachelor's degree in public relations can find staff positions with either an organization or a public relations firm.

More than 200 colleges and about 100 graduate schools offer degree programs or special courses in public relations. Many other colleges offer at least courses in the field. Public relations programs are sometimes administered by the journalism or communication departments of schools. In addition to courses in theory and techniques of public relations, interested individuals may study management and administration, organization, and practical applications and often specialize in areas such as business, government, and nonprofit organizations. Other preparation includes courses in advertising, communications, creative writing, journalism, and psychology.

Certification or Licensing

The Public Relations Society of America and the International Association of Business Communicators accredit public relations workers who have at least five years of experience in the field and pass a comprehensive examination. Such accreditation is a sign of competence in this field, although it is not a requirement for employment.

Other Requirements

Today's public relations specialist must be a businessperson first, both to understand how to perform successfully in business and to comprehend the needs and goals of the organization or client. Additionally, the public relations specialist needs to be a strong writer and speaker, with good interpersonal, leadership, and organizational skills.

EXPLORING

Almost any experience in working with other people will help you to develop strong interpersonal skills, which are crucial in public relations. The possibilities are almost endless. Summer work on a newspaper or trade paper or with a television station or film company may give insight into communications media. Working as a volunteer on a political campaign can help you to understand the ways in which people can be persuaded. Being selected as a page for the U.S. Congress or state legislature will help you grasp the fundamentals of government processes. A job in retail will help you to understand some of the principles of product presentation. A teaching job will develop your organization and presentation skills. These are just some of the jobs that will let you explore areas of public relations.

EMPLOYERS

Approximately 29,000 public relations specialists are employed in advertising and related industries in the United States. Public relations may be done for a corporation, retail business, service company, utility, association, nonprofit organization, or educational institution. Workers may be paid employees of the organization they represent or they may be part of a public relations firm that works for organizations on a contract basis. Others are involved in fund-raising or political campaigning.

Most PR firms are located in large cities that are centers of communications. Chicago, Los Angeles, New York, San Francisco, and Washington, D.C., are good places to start a search for a public relations job. Nevertheless, many opportunities exist in cities across the United States.

STARTING OUT

There is no clear-cut formula for getting a job in public relations. Individuals often enter the field after gaining preliminary experience in another occupation closely allied to the field, usually some segment of communications, and frequently, in journalism. Coming into public relations from newspaper work is still a recommended route. Another good method is to gain initial employment as a public relations trainee or intern, or as a clerk, secretary, or research assistant in a public relations department or a counseling firm.

ADVANCEMENT

In some large companies, an entry-level public relations specialist may start as a trainee in a formal training program for new employees. In others, new employees may be assigned to work that has a minimum of responsibility. They may assemble clippings or do rewrites on material that has already been accepted. They may make posters or assist in conducting polls or surveys, or compile reports from data submitted by others.

As workers acquire experience, they are given more responsibility. They write news releases, direct polls or surveys, or advance to writing speeches for company officials. Progress may seem to be slow, because some skills take a long time to master.

Some advance in responsibility and salary in the same firm in which they started. Others find that the path to advancement is to accept a more attractive position in another firm.

The goal of many public relations specialists is to open an independent office or to join an established consulting firm. To start an independent office requires a large outlay of capital and an established reputation in the field. However, those who are successful in operating their own consulting firms probably attain the greatest financial success in the public relations field.

EARNINGS

Public relations specialists employed in advertising and related industries had mean annual earnings of $60,330 in 2006, according to the U.S. Department of Labor. Salaries for all PR specialists ranged from less than $28,080 to more than $89,220.

Many PR workers receive a range of fringe benefits from corporations and agencies employing them, including bonus/incentive compensation, stock options, profit sharing/pension plans/401(k) programs, medical benefits, life insurance, financial planning, maternity/paternity leave, paid vacations, and family college tuition. Bonuses can range from 5 to 100 percent of base compensation and often are based on individual and/or company performance.

WORK ENVIRONMENT

Public relations specialists generally work in offices with adequate secretarial help, regular salary increases, and expense accounts. They are expected to make a good appearance in tasteful, conservative clothing. They must have social poise, and their conduct in their personal life is important to their firms or their clients. The public relations specialist may have to entertain business associates.

The PR specialist seldom works the conventional office hours for many weeks at a time; although the workweek may consist of 35 to 40 hours, these hours may be supplemented by evenings and even weekends when meetings must be attended and other special events covered. Time behind the desk may represent only a small part of the total working schedule. Travel is often an important and necessary part of the job.

The life of the PR worker is so greatly determined by the job that many consider this a disadvantage. Because the work is concerned with public opinion, it is often difficult to measure the results of performance and to sell the worth of a public relations program to an employer or client. Competition in the consulting field is keen, and if a firm loses an account, some of its personnel may be affected. The demands it makes for anonymity will be considered by some as one of the profession's less inviting aspects. Public relations involves much more hard work and a great deal less glamour than is popularly supposed.

OUTLOOK

Employment of public relations professionals in advertising and related industries is expected to grow much faster than the average for all occupations through 2016, according to the U.S. Department of Labor. Competition will be keen for beginning jobs in public relations because so many job seekers are enticed by the perceived glamour and appeal of the field; those with both education and experience will have an advantage.

Most large companies have some sort of public relations resource, either through their own staff or through the use of a firm of consultants. They are expected to expand their public relations activities and create many new jobs. More smaller companies are hiring public relations specialists, adding to the demand for these workers. Additionally, as a result of recent corporate scandals, more public relations specialists will be hired to help improve the images of companies and regain the trust of the public.

FOR MORE INFORMATION

For information on accreditation, contact
International Association of Business Communicators
One Hallidie Plaza, Suite 600
San Francisco, CA 94102-2842
Tel: 415-544-4700
http://www.iabc.com

For statistics, salary surveys, and information on accreditation and student membership, contact
Public Relations Society of America
33 Maiden Lane, 11th Floor
New York, NY 10038-5150
Tel: 212-460-1400
Email: prssa@prsa.org (student membership)
http://www.prsa.org

For information on program accreditation and professional development, contact
Canadian Public Relations Society
4195 Dundas Street West, Suite 346
Toronto, ON M8X 1Y4 Canada
Tel: 416-239-7034
Email: admin@cprs.ca
http://www.cprs.ca

Telemarketers

QUICK FACTS

School Subjects
Business
Speech

Personal Skills
Communication/ideas
Helping/teaching

Work Environment
Primarily indoors
Primarily one location

Minimum Education Level
High school diploma

Salary Range
$14,680 to $20,990 to
$38,430+

Certification or Licensing
None available

Outlook
Decline

DOT
299

GOE
10.04.01

NOC
5243

O*NET-SOC
41-9041.00

OVERVIEW

Telemarketers make and receive phone calls on behalf of a company to sell its goods, market its services, gather information, receive orders and complaints, and/or handle other miscellaneous business. According to the Direct Marketing Association, the activities most frequently performed by telemarketers are inputting mail orders and verifying names and addresses.

Telemarketing professionals might work directly for one company or for several companies that use the same service. In addition to selling, telemarketers place and receive calls to raise funds, conduct marketing research surveys, or raise public awareness. Accordingly, a wide variety of organizations in many industries employ telemarketers. There are currently 395,000 people who work part time or full time as telemarketers.

HISTORY

It is no exaggeration to say that the telephone has become an indispensable part of our daily lives. The speed of communicating by phone and the ability to reach the exact people with whom we want to speak have drastically changed the way business has been conducted over the past hundred years.

Since World War II, many companies have turned to marketing to expand business. Marketing involves finding the most likely customers for a product or service and then targeting those customers for sales, investment, or other business activity. A popular form of marketing is telemarketing, or the use of phone calls to sell a product or service, to find out about potential customers, to stay in touch with current customers, or to provide consumers with the most current information on new products and services. One of telemarketing's greatest strengths is that it allows callers direct contact with potential customers.

THE JOB

Telemarketers generally work for one of two types of businesses. Some telemarketers are part of the in-house staff of a company or corporation and make and receive calls on behalf of that company. Others work for a telemarketing service agency and make or receive calls for the clients of the agency. Telemarketing agencies are useful for companies that don't want to or can't keep a full-time telemarketing staff on the payroll or that need telemarketing services only occasionally. Both large corporations and small firms employ telemarketing agencies, which sometimes specialize in particular fields, such as fund-raising, product sales, and insurance.

Telemarketers are generally responsible for either handling incoming calls or placing calls to outside parties. Incoming calls may include requests for information or orders for an advertised product, such as clothing, magazines, appliances, or books. Telemarketers also staff the phones that handle toll-free, "800" numbers, which customers call to ask questions about the use of a product or to register complaints. Airline reservations, concert and sports tickets, and credit card problems are all transactions that can be handled by telemarketers. Newspapers often employ *classified ad clerks* to transcribe classified ads from callers. A person whose sole job is taking orders from callers over the phone is sometimes called an *order clerk*.

Telemarketers place outside calls for many purposes as well. One of the most important reasons for such calls is to sell products and services to consumers. The phone numbers of the people that telemarketers call usually come from a prepared list of previous customers, the phone book, reply cards from magazines, or a list purchased from another source. Sometimes randomly dialed "cold calls" are made. Once made, these calls often serve as a source of potential leads for the company's regular sales staff. A wide range of products—from newspaper subscriptions and credit cards to time-share resort condominiums and long-distance service—can be successfully sold in this way. Once a sale is made, the telemarketer records all necessary information, such as the buyer's name and address, product choices, and payment information, so that order fillers can prepare the product for shipment.

Cultural organizations, such as ballet and opera companies, public television stations, and theater troupes, use telemarketers to solicit subscriptions and donations. Charity fund-raising also relies heavily on telemarketing.

In addition to selling, telemarketers make calls for other reasons. They may conduct marketing surveys of consumers to discover the reasons for their buying decisions or what they like and dislike about a certain product. They may call to endorse a candidate in an upcoming election or tell citizens about an important vote in their city council. When making calls business-to-business, telemarketers may try to encourage attendance at important meetings, assist a company in recruitment and job placement, or collect demographic information for use in an advertising campaign.

When making outbound calls, telemarketers usually work from a prepared script that they must follow exactly. This is especially true of market research surveys because people need to be asked the same questions in the same way if the survey data are to be valid. Often when a customer tries to resist a sales pitch, the telemarketer will read a standard response that has been prepared in anticipation of potential objections. At other times, the telemarketer must rely on persuasive sales skills and quick thinking to win over the customer and make the sale. Telemarketers have to be a little more skillful when selling business-to-business because these

A telemarketer in a group call center talks with a potential customer. *(Daniel Karmann, dpa/Corbis)*

customers usually have a clear idea of the needs of their businesses and will ask specific questions.

Most telemarketers work at firms that are completely automated, allowing them to use virtually paperless systems. In addition, many telemarketing agencies use automatic call distribution systems that dispense calls evenly among employees for the fastest customer service possible. Through the use of database marketing and Internet registration services, firms can target markets even more accurately, thereby increasing the chances of successful sales calls.

REQUIREMENTS

High School

The skills and education you need to become a telemarketer depend in part on the firm for which you plan to work. A high school diploma is usually required for any type of position, while some employers hire only people who have earned college degrees.

Since you must be able to speak persuasively and listen to customers carefully, you will find classes in broadcasting, communications, drama, English, and speech particularly useful. Business and sales classes, as well as psychology and sociology, are also valuable. In addition, since many telemarketing positions require the use of computers for entering data, familiarity and experience with technology in general and data processing in particular are pluses.

Postsecondary Training

Although a college degree is not absolutely necessary for many telemarketing positions, some employers hire only college graduates. Since telemarketers sell and/or communicate over the telephone, college degrees in communications, drama, English, and speech are especially useful for those aspiring to the job of telemarketer. In addition, general business classes, such as advertising, marketing, and sales, are valuable. Also, courses in psychology and human behavior can help telemarketers gain insight to the wide variety of people that they often speak to during the course of a typical workday.

Other Requirements

If a telemarketer's phone calls focus on a complex product or service, as is the case with many business-to-business calls, people trained in the specific field involved may be hired and then instructed in telephone and sales techniques.

Even though their work is done over the phone, telemarketers must be able to deal well with other people. This work requires the ability to sense how customers are reacting, to keep them interested in the sales pitch, to listen carefully to their responses and complaints, and to react tactfully to impatient and sometimes hostile people. You must be able to balance a sensitivity to your company's concerns with the needs of the customer.

To succeed in telemarketing, you must have a warm, pleasant phone voice that conveys sincerity and confidence. You must be detail oriented as well. While on the phone, you have to take orders, get other important information, and fill out complete sales records, all of which requires an accurate and alert mind.

Many federal, state, and local laws have been enacted governing the sort of language and sales tactics that can be used with phone solicitation. Such legislation is intended to protect consumers from unscrupulous telemarketers operating phone scams. Telemarketers must be aware of these laws and conduct their phone sales in an honest and unambiguous manner. To bolster the industry's image in the eyes of the public, several professional organizations exist to further the cause of ethical and effective telemarketing.

EXPLORING

There are numerous ways to gain practice and poise in telemarketing. Many organizations use volunteer phone workers during campaigns and fund drives. One of the most visible of these is public television stations, which conduct fund-raising drives several times a year and are always looking for volunteer help to staff the phone banks. Other groups that routinely need volunteer telemarketers include local political campaigns, theaters and other arts groups, churches, schools, and nonprofit social organizations, such as crisis centers and inner-city recreation programs.

EMPLOYERS

Approximately 395,000 people work part time or full time as telemarketers. Work is available at a wide variety of establishments, from large multinational corporations, educational publishers, and government agencies to nonprofit organizations, retail catalog outlets, and service businesses. While jobs in telemarketing can be found nationwide, the cost of operating call centers varies, depending on their location. Some of the most expensive cities in which to operate call centers, for example, are New York, San Francisco, and Washington, D.C., while the least expensive cities include Columbia, South Carolina, and Mobile, Alabama. Large corporations often house their telemarketing centers in cities where both operating costs and salaries are low.

STARTING OUT

Agencies that hire telemarketers usually advertise for new employees in the classified section of newspapers, as well as on the Web. Another possible source of job leads is temporary employment agencies, many of which specialize in placing telemarketers with firms. Employers of telemarketers sometimes interview job applicants over the phone, judging a person's telephone voice, personality, demeanor, and assertiveness. Being prepared for such an interview before contacting an agency can make the difference between getting the job and having to continue to look.

Employees undergo a great deal of on-the-job training after they have been hired. Trainers instruct novice telemarketers on the use of equipment, characteristics of the product or service they will be selling, and proper sales techniques and listening skills. They rehearse the trainees on the script that has been prepared and guide them through some practice calls.

ADVANCEMENT

Within telemarketing agencies, employees can advance to jobs as *telemarketing managers.* These professionals have a variety of responsibilities, including preparing reports, writing telephone scripts, setting goals and objectives, implementing new service programs, monitoring and analyzing inquiries and complaints, recruiting, scheduling, and training. Along with these responsibilities, telemarketing managers sometimes enjoy rapidly increasing salaries because they can often earn commissions on the net sales achieved by the agency.

Some telemarketers move into telephone sales training, either with agencies or as independent consultants. Experienced telemarketers can sometimes find new jobs with higher-paying firms, while still others start their own telemarketing agencies.

EARNINGS

Telemarketers' earnings vary with the type of work they do. For part-time phone solicitors making basic calls to consumers, the pay can range from the minimum wage to around $8 per hour. Pay may be higher for those who deliver more elaborate sales presentations, work weekends, or make business-to-business calls. As telemarketers gain experience and skills, their pay scales rise. According to the U.S. Department of Labor, median annual earnings of telemarketers were $20,990 in 2006. Salaries ranged from less than $14,680 to more than $38,430.

Telemarketing workers also frequently enjoy such employee benefits as health and life insurance, paid vacation and sick days, and profit sharing. With such a wide range of organizations for which telemarketers can work, the benefits offered depend entirely on the employer.

WORK ENVIRONMENT

The offices in which telemarketers work can range from the very basic, with standard phones and desks, to the highly advanced, with computer terminals, the latest in communications technology, and machines that automatically dial numbers from a database. There may be just four or five telemarketers in a smaller office or more than 100 working at a larger office. While the work is not strenuous, it can be very repetitive. The amount of supervision depends on the employer and the region of the country. California and a few other states, for example, have laws that prohibit recording calls or monitoring by supervisors unless both the telemarketer and the person being called are aware of it.

Telemarketing requires many hours of sitting and talking on the phone. Customer rejections, which range from polite to rude, can cause a great deal of stress. As a result, many telemarketers work only four- or five-hour shifts. Telemarketing is an ideal job for people looking for part-time work because workweeks generally run from 24 to 30 hours. Because many agencies need staff at unusual hours, telemarketers are often able to find positions offering schedules that match their lifestyles. Many agencies require staffing 24 hours a day to handle such calls as airline reservations and reports of stolen credit cards. Telemarketers who make business-to-business calls work during normal business hours, while those who call consumers make most of their calls in the evening and on weekends, when more people are at home.

OUTLOOK

The U.S. Department of Labor predicts that employment of telemarketers (including those employed in advertising and related industries) will decline due to the establishment of the National Do Not Call Registry by the Federal Trade Commission. The registry, which allows people to place their phone numbers on a do not call list, severely limits the ability of telemarketers to contact potential customers without their consent. Calls from or on behalf of telephone surveyors, charities, and political organizations are still permitted.

Telemarketers will still be needed to contact individuals who have not placed their telephone numbers on do not call lists. Those who assist customers via toll-free "800" numbers, as well as those who process orders for a variety of products and services, will still be needed. Turnover is high in this field due to the low pay and high stress, which will also create opportunities as workers leave the field for other occupations.

FOR MORE INFORMATION

The AMA is an internal professional society of individual members with an interest in the practice, study, and teaching of marketing.
American Marketing Association (AMA)
311 South Wacker Drive, Suite 5800
Chicago, IL 60606-6629
Tel: 800-262-1150
http://www.marketingpower.com

For the Customer Service Newsletter *and other resources about customer service, contact*
Customer Service Group
712 Main Street, Suite 187B
Boonton, NJ 07005-1469
Tel: 800-232-4317
http://www.customerservicegroup.com

The DMA is the largest trade association for individuals interested in database marketing.
Direct Marketing Association (DMA)
1120 Avenue of the Americas
New York, NY 10036-6700
Tel: 212-768-7277
http://www.the-dma.org

Index

Entries in **boldface** indicate main articles.